Dining in the Smoky Mountain Mist

To Sherold —
This is my favorite cookbook —
hope you'll enjoy!
Love Aunt

Happy Birthday —
James, Aunt, Dan, Christe

Dining in
the Smoky
Mountain Mist

A COLLECTION OF SEASONAL DELIGHTS FROM THE JUNIOR LEAGUE OF KNOXVILLE

First Edition
First Printing 1995
30,000

Copyright© 1995
The Junior League of Knoxville, Tennessee

Library of Congress Number: 95-61541
ISBN: 0-9608174-2-5

Manufactured in the United States of America by
Favorite Recipes® Press
2451 Atrium Way
Nashville, Tennessee 37214

*Our thanks to the many members who have contributed their favorite recipes
to **Dining in the Smoky Mountain Mist**. Some liberties have been taken
with the original recipes to ensure consistency of form.*

All proceeds from the sale of
Dining in the Smoky Mountain Mist
*are returned to the community through the
Junior League of Knoxville's projects.*

Additional copies of ***Dining in the Smoky Mountain Mist*** may be
obtained by writing:
The Junior League of Knoxville
Cookbook Committee
P.O. Box 11632
Knoxville, Tennessee 37939
(423) 523-0350

Mission Statement

The Junior League of Knoxville is an organization of women committed to promoting voluntarism and to improving the community through effective action and leadership of trained volunteers. Its purpose is exclusively educational and charitable.

Vision Statement

The Junior League of Knoxville will significantly improve the quality of life in our community by focusing our resources on critical needs of children and families and by providing a legacy of trained volunteers.

Table of Contents

Tints of Spring

Shades of Summer

Harvest Hues

Tones of Winter

Napkins, Knives & Knoxville

Thank You

Attitude is important in making acquaintance of the Smokies. They do not present the barren timberline heights or the perpetually snow-capped summits of some other mountain ranges. Their green cover lends them an amiable aura of easy accessibility. But the riches of the Great Smokies have been a long time a-gathering, and they do not yield instantly to the impatient visitor.

—*Wilma Dykeman*
Explorations

Wilma Dykeman

Our sincere gratitude goes to Wilma Dykeman, renowned for her works depicting the people, women, and history of Appalachia and Tennessee, for her participation in this project. Her works, *Explorations*, and *Tennessee, A History,* are quoted extensively in this book. Her descriptive prose has perfectly served as the thread that ties the various elements of this work together. For this we are truly thankful.

Wilma Dykeman's 17 books include novels, histories, biographies, essays, social commentary, and a volume for *TIME-LIFE*.

Wilma's articles have appeared in *The New York Times Magazine, Harper's New Republic, Fortune, U.S. News & World Report,* and many other magazines.

A widely known lecturer, Wilma speaks across the United States, has received numerous literary and civic awards, and serves on several educational, financial, and conservation boards.

Two sons and two grandchildren are her special joy.

Missy Flaherty

A heartfelt thank you is due Missy Flaherty, photographer, for all of her hard work and dedication to the photographic elements of this book. She artfully captured both the feel and beauty of the East Tennessee landscape and its seasons, lifestyle, and moments that make life in this part of the country so very special. Her photographs taken at The Inn at Blackberry Farm provided the background for a magnificent cover shot.

For Missy Flaherty, Knoxville-based commercial and editorial photographer, the giving in this cookbook has been a labor of love.

Some photographs, including the cover, were shot at sunrise, some at dusk. All are of this region of East Tennessee and each one brought an enriching experience into Missy's life.

Missy's greatest blessing and source of joy is her own family life shared with her husband, Frank, and their two sons, Patrick and Preston.

Introduction

Dinner with friends, meals with family, parties with casual acquaintances—wherever, whenever food is served, there is another kind of nourishment present or absent. Is conversation on your menu?

No doctor's prescription or analyst's survey is necessary to tell us that the mood set at a meal is as important as the way the places are set. The memories most of us have of family gatherings—on important holidays or in daily routines—grow from the good or ill temper, the stimulation or boredom, the haste or relaxation of those who created the atmosphere, as well as those who created the food. We are reminded in Proverbs, "Better a dinner of herbs where love is than a stalled ox and hatred therewith."

One of our country's leaders several years ago shared insight into an important influence in his family's life when he recollected that the conversation, the ideas, the differences of opinion that his father encouraged around the dinner table helped prepare him to become president of the United States.

As for our memories of elegant dinner parties, they glow with special pleasure when we recall both a feast of delectable cuisine and a ferment of spirited conversation. This means, of course, that on such occasions there are guests who are interesting—not necessarily famous, but interesting because of their work, their wit, their attentiveness and insight into the world around them.

And then there are the guests who are interested—who can listen to the famous and the glamorous and ask the right questions, hang on every word of the raconteur. An internationally acclaimed hostess once advised that rule number one for a successful dinner party was to remember that stars of some kind are desirable, but there must also be satellites.

I would interpret that in a way that could apply to every occasion when we break bread together: to become an interesting host or hostess or guest, parent or child or family member, it is necessary first to be interested in others.

Arranging a menu of conversational delicacies, then, it might be useful to consider:

the entree, perhaps a guest or two with rich knowledge, even discovery, in a special field of work or profession, be it painting or politics, medicine or forestry or cybernetics, it's the passion of their dedication that is fulfilling;

a tossed salad of friends who are the alert and lively satellites bringing their own flavor to the occasion;

the sparkle of at least one witty participant whose observations sprinkle salt and spice to add savor to the occasion;

as dessert, the delicate sweetness of the words of that friend who is a steadfast optimist and always assures her hostess the next morning that "it was a wonderful party"; or dessert may be the reminder of a child who tells you, years later, that that special meal "you used to make" has never been forgotten, in part because of the "talks we had."

Yes, our words, our conversation also provide nourishment, add another dimension to the wish

bon appetit!

—Wilma Dykeman

Junior League of Knoxville
75 Years of Community Service

To commemorate our 75th anniversary, the Junior League of Knoxville has gathered its resources to provide a culinary insight and historical perspective of our League.

One of the oldest Leagues in the South, the Junior League of Knoxville began as The Girls' Relief Corps in October of 1917. War work and community service were the primary aims for the organization. Volunteers assisted the American Red Cross in rolling bandages, sewing and staffing canteens, meeting troop trains at Knoxville's Southern Station, and delivering baskets of food to the needy. After four years of welfare work, in 1921 The Girls' Relief Corps became the Junior League of Knoxville, and so began our seventy-five year history.

As early as the 1920s, League members raised over $20,000 to build a preventorium at the Beverly Hills Tuberculous Hospital and to establish the Home for Friendless Babies. The Home grew into the Knoxville Children's Bureau and later became the Child and Family Services Agency. Both projects were designed to provide care for underprivileged children. By 1929, the League had taken over financial support and administrative control of the Dale Avenue Settlement House. For nine years, the League alone financed and staffed the Settlement House; it later became part of the Community Chest budget. The League supported the settlement house through volunteers and fund raising until 1959. Years later, the property at Dale Avenue Settlement House was sold to the City of Knoxville for right of way. The remaining land was sold to the State of Tennessee. The money was used to purchase the Junior League headquarters in December of 1979.

During the 1930s, economic depression caused many hardships for the Knoxville community. The Junior League provided volunteers for four branch libraries of the city system that would have closed for lack of personnel. The library service continued until a new city budget provided for staff librarians. League members also conducted a survey for the Knoxville Association of the Blind and worked with the blind as part of their community service. In 1938, the Hospital Committee first established a rolling library for the patients at Fort Sanders Hospital. During that same year, the Community Chest was organized with the League's support. In 1953, the Community Chest became the United Fund and the League was responsible for the residential division of the drive for many years.

The War years brought out a new level of commitment in the League. In addition to regular volunteer jobs, members devoted their time to the American Red Cross, The Office of Civilian Defense, War Bond Drives, and the Cancer Drive. Volunteer efforts of the late 1940s yielded support for a Child Guidance Clinic and a newly established Mental Health Center. To top off these years of extraordinary activity, the creativity of League members was at a high as they wrote, acted out, and broadcasted over WBIR, WROL, and WNOX radio a series of award-winning children's stories, to the delight of Knoxville's youth.

In 1952, a presentation of "The Women" sparked the idea of a joint community-university theater, an idea which grew into the increasingly popular Carousal Theater. In June of that same year, the Bargain Box Thrift Shop was born. Throughout its thirty-five years of operation, League and community members, as well as local merchants provided "attractive merchandise and wearing apparel at reasonable prices so that families (were) able to dress for less." This enormously successful shop, catering to the underprivileged, generated seventy-five percent of the League's operating budget, funding all other League-sponsored activities. In April of 1986 the League held a new fund-raising event—Bag A Bargain—in the Jacobs building at the Knoxville Fairgrounds. The first annual Bag A Bargain was a huge success, with customers lined around the building hours before we were scheduled to open. The Bag A Bargain, a flea market sale, continues to provide both a service to the community as well as valuable funds to support the League's many projects.

Funds from the original Bargain Box were used in 1955 to support the East Tennessee Hearing and Speech Center. A new building was dedicated to the Hearing and Speech Center in the fall of 1959. The center later merged with the University of Tennessee. The Dogwood Arts Festival, co-sponsored with the Knoxville Chamber of Commerce and the Knoxville Junior League, was begun in 1960. During the spring of 1965, an award was given to the League by the National Recreational Association for Services to the Dogwood Arts Festival. The arts and art appreciation continued to be a focus area, with League volunteers supporting projects such as Arts to the Schools and the Children's Arts Program. The Children's Arts Program was created in cooperation with the Tennessee Arts Commission and the Dulin Art Gallery.

Education on the dangers of drug and alcohol abuse made up much of the League's efforts during the early part of the 1970s. Films were shown to grade school children and programs were implemented with the PTA and the Kiwanis Clubs. The seventies also brought about two important and extremely successful fund raisers for the League's expanding community commitments—The Favorite Shops of Christmas held in 1977-78 and the printing of the first Junior League cookbook, "The Pear Tree." At the request of the Downtown Rotary Club, the Choral Group was recognized by the mayor, who proclaimed the week of April 11, 1977, as Junior League Choral Group Week.

The decade of the 1980s was a busy time for active members as projects continued to expand into areas connected with children and education. Peer Tutoring, Parent Education, Traveling Trunks, and Adopt A School were just some of the many community activities. Peer Tutoring was on the program of the National Adopt A School conference. The League was honored with the Volunteer of the Year award from the Social Workers' Association, and the Knoxville Volunteer Coordinating Center was accepted as a United Way agency. The organization continued its relationship with the Knoxville Museum of Art and developed new relationships with Ijams Nature Center and the newly developed Center School.

Collaborative efforts with other agencies mark the 1990s as the membership looks for new ways to use their volunteers and

monies to support a constantly growing community. A community-wide effort to meet the health needs of the working poor was made through the development of the *InterFaith Health Clinic*. League programs supported the Center School, addressing the high school dropout issue, and members became Court Appointed Special Advocates serving children in the juvenile justice system. The Signature Project was started to mark seventy-five years of community service and developed into "Knoxville Connects," a collaborative effort of five different community agencies working together to meet the needs of children and families.

The Junior League of Knoxville has a remarkable history of continuous growth and steadfast commitment to the mission of community service. Despite obstacles in the past, the organization has remained sensitive to the ever-changing needs of Knoxville's surrounding community. The women of the organization have lived the vision recently developed and adopted by the Association of Junior Leagues. For seventy-five years, they have "through the power of their association embraced diverse perspectives, built partnerships, and inspired shared solutions."

This book is dedicated to members of the Junior League everywhere who gave, and continue to give, so willingly of their time, energy, and creativity to better their communities throughout the world.

In 1921, the Junior League of Knoxville had 58 active members and an annual budget of $910.75.

After having netted a total of $1,000.00 in proceeds from the 1930-31 year Annual Charity Ball (quite a feat considering the economy of the time), the bank in which this sum was held COLLAPSED.

In the 1935-36 year, each Provisional or Active League member was required to pay a $0.50 fine for not attending a regular business meeting without having an adequate excuse. By 1949-50, that fine had become $1.00.

1936 was the first year that the Junior League of Knoxville abolished its original "Hour," or "Point," system and began monitoring volunteer commitment by "Placement." This meant that, for the first time, League members had a choice in their volunteer efforts.

In 1941, the Charity Ball celebrated its 20th Anniversary, and the Grand Prizes given away were Defense Bonds.

The Junior League of Knoxville President, serving as Chairman of the Volunteer Office of the Office of Civil Defense, was asked to christen the frigate USS Knoxville in 1943.

"The Ladies in Blue" was the name given to the members of the Children's Hospital Auxiliary founded by an organization of League Sustainers in 1956.

1960 was the first year that the Junior League of Knoxville deemed it necessary and beneficial to the membership to begin holding meetings during the evening.

League year 1974-75 was the first year the Junior League of Knoxville began a program of "Management by Objectives" in its internal (League) and external (community) dealings.

11

Tints of Spring

APPETIZERS

BREADS

BRUNCH

Last —

first, best, most

welcome — there are

people we know

who harbor springtime

and share its energy

throughout their lives.

They see each morning

afresh. They welcome

new beginnings.

—*Wilma Dykeman*
Explorations

Appetizers

There are

"appetizer" people

and "dessert" people . . .

Those who savor the salt

and tang and variety

of hors d'oeuvres are often

too stuffed to enjoy

the riches of dessert.

—*Wilma Dykeman*
Explorations

Tints of Spring

Rave reviews! This is a bright, colorful dish— adorn with a sliced tomato in the shape of a flower with basil as the leaves.

Bruschetta Romano

Ingredients

2	pounds plum tomatoes, chopped
1	small red onion, chopped
1	cup packed chopped fresh basil
4	cloves of garlic, minced
3	anchovies, finely chopped
1¼	tablespoons salt
1¼	tablespoons white pepper
1	teaspoon oregano
1¼	cups extra-virgin olive oil
2	loaves French bread, thinly sliced
½	cup freshly grated Romano cheese

❧ Combine the tomatoes, onion, basil, garlic, anchovies, salt, white pepper, oregano and olive oil in a large bowl. Chill, covered, in the refrigerator for 4 hours, stirring occasionally.

❧ Let the bruschetta topping stand at room temperature for 30 minutes before serving.

❧ Place the bread slices on baking sheets.

❧ Bake at 250 degrees for 5 to 10 minutes or until light brown. Sprinkle the cheese over the warm toast. Serve with bruschetta topping.

yields twelve servings

Cheese Straws

Ingredients

1	pound sharp Cheddar cheese, shredded
3	cups sifted flour
1	cup margarine, softened
1	teaspoon salt
2	tablespoons Worcestershire sauce
1	tablespoon paprika
½	teaspoon red pepper

Combine the cheese with flour, margarine, salt, Worcestershire sauce, paprika and red pepper in a bowl; mix well. Spoon the mixture into a cookie press. Press into desired shapes on an ungreased baking sheet.

Bake at 375 degrees on the bottom rack of the oven for 5 minutes. Move to the top rack. Bake for 5 minutes longer or until edges are brown. Cool on the baking sheet for several minutes. Remove to a wire rack to cool completely.

yields forty-eight appetizers

Crab-Stuffed Mushrooms

Ingredients

12	large fresh mushrooms
1	(6-ounce) can lump crab meat, drained
¼	cup grated Parmesan cheese
¼	cup thinly sliced green onions
2	tablespoons fat-free mayonnaise
1	teaspoon each Worcestershire sauce and Dijon mustard
¼	teaspoon white pepper

Rinse the mushrooms; pat dry with paper towels. Remove the stems, reserving the caps. Chop enough of the stems to measure 1 cup.

Place the chopped stems in a small skillet coated with nonstick cooking spray. Cook, covered, over medium heat for 5 minutes. Remove from the heat. Stir in the crab meat, Parmesan cheese, green onions, mayonnaise, Worcestershire sauce, mustard and pepper; mix well. Spoon the mixture into the mushroom caps. Place the filled caps on a baking pan coated with nonstick cooking spray.

Bake at 350 degrees for 15 minutes or until lightly browned.

yields twelve appetizers

A true southern tradition for those times when friends "come a calling!" These cheese straws keep forever and are the perfect finger food to serve to "proper southern ladies."

Tints of Spring

Egg Rolls

Ingredients

2	tablespoons vegetable oil
3	cups shredded cabbage
½	cup chopped onion
½	cup finely chopped celery
8	ounces bamboo shoots, chopped
8	ounces water chestnuts, chopped
1	cup each shredded carrots and bean sprouts
3½	pounds cooked pork, finely chopped
1½	cups finely chopped cooked chicken
8	ounces peeled cooked popcorn shrimp
¼	cup soy sauce
¼	teaspoon each dry mustard and ginger
½	cup cornstarch
½	cup water
1	(2-pound) package egg roll wrappers
	Vegetable oil for frying

Heat 2 tablespoons oil in a wok. Stir-fry the cabbage, onion and celery in the h
oil for 2 minutes. Remove from heat. Combine the stir-fried vegetables with bamboo
shoots, water chestnuts, carrots, bean sprouts, pork, chicken, shrimp, soy sauce, must
and ginger in a bowl.

Combine the cornstarch and water in a small bowl. Set aside.

Spoon 3 tablespoonfuls of the egg roll filling in the center of each egg roll
wrapper. Fold the top corner of the wrapper over the filling, tucking tip of corner und
filling. Fold left and right corners over filling. Brush the exposed corner with cornstar
mixture; roll tightly and press to seal.

Heat 1 to 2 inches oil in a wok. Fry egg rolls 2 at a time in the hot oil for 45
seconds on each side, adding additional oil as needed; drain.

yields twenty-four appetizers

Focaccia Tomato Pie

Ingredients

	Fresh summer tomatoes, coarsely chopped
⅓	cup olive oil
⅔	cup balsamic vinegar
1	focaccia loaf
	Salt and pepper to taste

Place the tomatoes in a large shallow dish. Sprinkle with the olive oil and vinegar. Marinate at room temperature for 30 minutes or longer.

Place the focaccia on a baking sheet. Bake at 350 degrees for 10 minutes. Place on a large serving plate and cut into thin wedges with pizza cutter. Spoon the tomatoes over the focaccia. Serve immediately.

May sprinkle focaccia with grated Parmesan cheese before baking.

yields sixteen appetizers

Goat Cheese with Olives and Sun-Dried Tomatoes

Ingredients

1	(8-ounce) jar oil-pack sun-dried tomatoes
2	large cloves of garlic, cut into halves
⅔	cup Kalamata olives, pitted, chopped
12	ounces Montrachet cheese, sliced
1	baguette French bread, sliced
	Fresh basil sprigs

Combine the undrained tomatoes and garlic in the bowl of a food processor. Process until smooth. Combine with the olives in a small serving bowl. Place the bowl in the center of a serving platter. Arrange the cheese slices and bread around the bowl. Garnish with fresh basil sprigs. Top each bread slice with cheese and tomato mixture to serve.

yields twenty-four appetizers

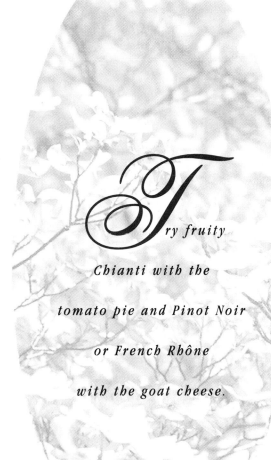

Try fruity Chianti with the tomato pie and Pinot Noir or French Rhône with the goat cheese.

Tints of Spring

A mixed
arrangement of lilies,
stock, bells of Ireland and
larkspur in a favorite
vase, along with asparagus
fern, adds great color
to a casual party.

Spinach Pastry Roll-Ups

Ingredients

2	(10-ounce) packages frozen spinach, thawed, drained
1	egg, beaten
1	cup crumbled feta cheese
½	cup cottage cheese
½	cup chopped green onions
1½	teaspoons (or more) dill
	Pepper to taste
2	sheets puff pastry, thawed
1	tablespoon water
1	egg, beaten

Combine the spinach, 1 egg, feta cheese, cottage cheese, green onions, dill and pepper in a bowl; mix well.

Unroll 1 sheet of the puff pastry on a floured surface. Place ½ of the spinach mixture along the long side of each pastry sheet. Roll to enclose filling, tucking in the sides. Place seam side down on a baking sheet coated with nonstick baking spray. Mix tablespoon water with the remaining beaten egg in a small bowl. Brush a portion of the egg wash over the egg rolls. Repeat the procedure with the remaining pastry sheet, spinach filling and egg wash.

Bake at 350 degrees for 45 to 60 minutes or until brown. Cool on baking sheet for several minutes. Cut into slices. Serve warm or at room temperature.

May be frozen, thawed and baked at 300 degrees until brown.

yields twenty-four appetizers

Artichoke Dip

Ingredients

1	(14-ounce) can artichoke hearts, drained, chopped
1	(6-ounce) can marinated artichoke hearts, drained, chopped
1	(4-ounce) can green chiles, drained, chopped
6	tablespoons mayonnaise
2	cups shredded Cheddar cheese

❧ Combine the artichoke hearts, green chiles, mayonnaise and cheese in a bowl. Spoon into a greased 1½-quart baking dish.

❧ Bake at 350 degrees for 20 minutes.

❧ Serve hot with corn chips, Triscuits or assorted crackers.

yields five cups

Sugar-and-Spice Pecans

Ingredients

1	cup sugar
1	tablespoon cinnamon
2	teaspoons nutmeg
½	teaspoon salt
2	egg whites, at room temperature
3	tablespoons water
5	cups pecan halves

❧ Mix the sugar, cinnamon, nutmeg and salt in a bowl.

❧ Beat the egg whites with water in a mixer bowl until soft peaks form. Add the sugar mixture 1 tablespoonful at a time, beating until stiff. Fold in the pecan halves. Remove pecan halves to a greased 10x15-inch baking pan, using a slotted spoon.

❧ Bake at 300 degrees for 30 minutes, stirring every 10 minutes. Let stand to cool. Store in an airtight container.

yields five cups

*R*educe the calories in Artichoke Dip by using regular canned artichoke hearts rather than the marinated ones. Also, low-fat mayonnaise may be substituted.

Tints of Spring

Black Bean Dip

Ingredients

1½	cups frozen Shoe Peg corn, without sauce
1½	(15-ounce) cans black beans, drained
¾	cup chopped red onion
¾	cup chopped red bell pepper
2	large jalapeños, chopped
½	cup balsamic vinegar
⅓	cup olive oil
1½	tablespoons Dijon mustard
¼	cup chopped parsley
	Salt and pepper to taste

❧ Cook the corn for 5 minutes using package directions; drain.

❧ Combine the corn with black beans, onion, red pepper, jalapeños, vinegar, olive oil, mustard, parsley, salt and pepper in a bowl; mix well.

❧ Chill, covered, in refrigerator for up to 5 days. Spoon into a serving dish and serve with tortilla chips.

yields seven cups

Baked Crab Dip

Ingredients

8	ounces cream cheese, softened
3	tablespoons milk
1	tablespoon finely chopped onion
¼	teaspoon prepared horseradish
	Dash of garlic powder
4	ounces fresh crab meat
2	tablespoons grated Parmesan cheese
1	tablespoon chopped green onions

❧ Combine the cream cheese, milk, onion, horseradish and garlic powder in a bowl; mix well. Fold in crab meat. Spoon into a lightly greased baking dish.

❧ Bake at 400 degrees for 20 minutes. Sprinkle with Parmesan cheese and green onions. Serve with crackers or tortilla chips.

yields one and one-half cups

Cheddar Cheese Ring

Ingredients

16	ounces mild Cheddar cheese, shredded
16	ounces sharp Cheddar cheese, shredded
3	cups mayonnaise
2	cups chopped pecans
2	teaspoons cayenne pepper
2	cups leaf lettuce
1	(10-ounce) jar fruit preserves

Combine the cheeses, mayonnaise, pecans and cayenne in a bowl; mix well. Press the mixture into a greased 10-cup ring mold. Chill, covered, in refrigerator for 8 hours or longer.

Invert onto a lettuce-lined serving plate 1 hour before serving time. Spoon the preserves into a small serving bowl; place in the center of the ring. Serve with assorted crackers.

yields nine cups

Herb Cheese Spread

Ingredients

1	(12-ounce) package Havarti cheese
1	sheet frozen puff pastry, thawed
1	teaspoon Dijon mustard
1	teaspoon parsley flakes
½	teaspoon chives
¼	teaspoon dillweed
¼	teaspoon basil
1	egg, beaten

Place the cheese in the center of the puff pastry. Spread mustard over the top. Sprinkle with the parsley flakes, chives, dillweed and basil. Fold the pastry to enclose the filling, sealing the edges. Place seam side down on a greased baking sheet. Brush the tops with a portion of the beaten egg. Chill in refrigerator for 30 minutes.

Bake at 375 degrees for 20 minutes. Brush with the remaining beaten egg. Bake for 10 minutes longer. Serve warm with crackers and sliced apples.

yields twelve servings

*G*ather a collection of brochures from favorite services and local shops, a map and tour book for the area, and maybe even a gift certificate—wrap with a food gift in a decorative basket to welcome new neighbors.

Italian Torta

Ingredients

8	ounces pine nuts, chopped
1	tablespoon melted butter
	Salt to taste
24	ounces cream cheese, softened
2	cups butter, softened
⅓	cup prepared pesto
2	tablespoons sun-dried tomato purée

Place the pine nuts in a shallow baking pan; drizzle with 1 tablespoon melted butter and sprinkle with salt.

Bake at 350 degrees for 5 minutes or until toasted.

Line a 5x9-inch loaf pan with plastic wrap, extending additional wrap over the sides of pan.

Blend the cream cheese and butter in a bowl. Spread a ½-inch layer of cream cheese mixture in the prepared loaf pan. Layer half the pine nuts, ¼ of the remaining cream cheese mixture, pesto, ¼ of the cream cheese mixture, ½ of the pine nuts, ¼ of the cream cheese mixture, tomato purée and remaining ¼ of the cream cheese mixture in the loaf pan. Fold extra plastic wrap over layers, pressing gently to compact the layers. Chill in refrigerator.

Unmold the torta onto serving plate, removing the plastic wrap. Garnish with fresh basil leaves and tomato rose. Serve with crackers.

yields sixteen servings

Mushroom Pâté

Ingredients

8	ounces fresh mushrooms, finely chopped
¼	cup melted butter
1½	teaspoons minced garlic
¼	cup finely chopped scallion
⅓	cup chicken stock
4	ounces cream cheese, softened
2	tablespoons chopped green onion tops
	Salt and freshly ground pepper to taste

Sauté the mushrooms in 2 tablespoons of the butter in a skillet for 2 minutes. Add the garlic and scallion. Sauté for 1 minute longer. Add the chicken stock.

Cook over medium heat for 4 to 5 minutes or until the liquid is absorbed, stirring occasionally. Let stand until cooled to room temperature.

Combine the remaining 2 tablespoons butter, cream cheese, green onion tops, salt and pepper in bowl; mix well. Stir in the sautéed mixture. Spoon into a serving bowl. Garnish with parsley or a green onion.

Chill, covered, in refrigerator. Serve with water crackers.

yields one and one-half cups

Adorn the platter with cut pansies around the pâté to add color and liven up the look of any pâté.

Tints of Spring

Place the molded Salmon Pâté onto a decorative platter layered with fresh greens for color. Garnish the pâté with paper-thin slices of cucumber layered over one another to create the effect of gills. Use a green olive for the eye. Almonds may also be used for the gills to create a different look.

Salmon Pâté

Ingredients

1	(8-ounce) salmon fillet
¼	cup soy sauce
1	tablespoon vegetable oil
1	envelope onion soup mix
½	cup white wine
½	cup water
8	ounces cream cheese, softened
1	tablespoon lemon juice

Place the salmon in a shallow bowl and pour the soy sauce over the top. Marinate, covered, in refrigerator for several hours; drain.

Cook the salmon in the oil in a skillet over medium heat for several minutes. Add the onion soup mix, white wine and water. Cook just until the salmon is firm to the touch and flakes easily. Remove the salmon with a slotted spoon, reserving the pan drippings. Let stand until cool. Break the salmon into chunks.

Combine the pan drippings with cream cheese and lemon juice in a bowl; mix well. Stir in the salmon. Spoon the mixture into a greased fish-shape mold.

Chill, covered, in refrigerator for several hours. Unmold onto a lettuce-lined serving plate. Serve with assorted crackers.

yields twelve servings

Shepherd Loaf

Ingredients

1	large round loaf French bread
3	(3-ounce) cans minced clams
16	ounces cream cheese, softened
6	drops of Tabasco sauce
2	teaspoons chopped green onions
2	teaspoons lemon juice
2	teaspoons chopped parsley
2	teaspoons Worcestershire sauce

Slice off the top of the bread, reserving the top. Scoop out the center of the bread, leaving a ½-inch shell. Cut center into cubes to use for dipping.

Drain 2 cans of the clams. Combine with undrained clams, cream cheese, Tabasco sauce, green onions, lemon juice, parsley and Worcestershire sauce in a bowl; mix well. Spoon into the bread shell; replace the reserved top. Wrap in foil; place on a baking sheet.

Bake at 250 degrees for 2 hours or until heated through. Remove foil; place on serving dish. Serve with bread cubes for dipping.

May be frozen and baked for an additional hour.

yields sixteen servings

Breads

*A*nd the bread!

Biscuits light and flaky,

ready to soak butter and

blackberry jam or grape jelly

or orange marmalade to a melted

sweetness. Rolls so tempting

in their aroma that the reality

of their luscious lightness

seemed almost an anticlimax

to the anticipation.

—Wilma Dykeman
Explorations

Tints of Spring

*F*or 100 years

the White Lily flour mills

have been considered

by many to produce

the finest baking flour

in the country.

Famous White Lily Biscuits

Ingredients

2   cups White Lily self-rising flour

¼   cup shortening (not a liquid)

⅔   (to ¾) cup milk

❧ Combine the flour and shortening in a bowl. Cut in the shortening with a pastry blender until the mixture resembles coarse crumbs. Do not blend completely or the biscuits will be mealy. Push the mixture gently to the side, forming a well in the center. Add the milk, blending with a fork until the dough leaves the side of the bowl. Do not over mix. Turn the dough out onto a lightly floured surface.

❧ Knead gently for only 10 to 12 strokes. Pat or roll the dough to ¼-inch thickness. Cut with a 2-inch or 2½-inch biscuit cutter, dipping the cutter into flour between cuts. Place the biscuits on an ungreased baking sheet.

❧ Bake at 500 degrees for 6 to 8 minutes or until golden brown.

yields eight to twelve biscuits

Since the 1850's, when a woman's standing in her neighborhood was often determined by the quality of baking she produced from her heavy iron cookstove, Knoxville's bakers have consistently demanded an ever-finer quality of flour. The White Lily Food Company has risen to the occasion for more than one hundred years.

As Suzanne Hamlin wrote in **The New York Daily News**, "Warning: Knowing how to turn out great biscuits is like having a swimming pool; you'll make a lot of new friends—fast. And, take a tip from the South: If you're unmarried, take up biscuits."

Aloha Bread

Ingredients

3	cups flour
2	cups sugar
1	teaspoon baking soda
1	teaspoon salt
1	teaspoon cinnamon
1	cup finely chopped pecans
3	eggs, beaten
1½	cups vegetable oil
2	cups mashed bananas (4 medium)
1	(8-ounce) can crushed pineapple, drained
2	teaspoons vanilla extract

❧ Mix the flour, sugar, baking soda, salt and cinnamon in a bowl. Stir in the pecans.

❧ Combine the eggs, oil, bananas, pineapple and vanilla in a bowl. Stir in the dry ingredients just until moistened. Spoon the batter into 2 greased and floured 5x9-inch loaf pans.

❧ Bake at 350 degrees for 1 hour and 5 minutes or until the loaves test done. Cool in the pans for 10 minutes; remove to wire racks to cool completely.

yields two loaves

*H*ome *Sweet Tennessee!*

Everyone loves fresh bread. Stack a large flower basket high with a selection of different traditional loaves: Aloha Bread, Corn Bread, Swedish Vittebröd, the Best Bread in the World, Pepperoni Bread . . . whatever! Wrap each in colorful cloth napkins tied with ribbon.

Tints of Spring

Banana Date Bread

Ingredients

1½	cups butter, softened
1	cup sugar
2	eggs, beaten
3	medium bananas, mashed
2	cups flour
1	teaspoon salt
½	teaspoon baking soda
½	(8-ounce) package chopped dates
1	cup chopped pecans

Cream the butter and sugar in a mixer bowl until light and fluffy. Add the eggs; mix well. Stir in the mashed bananas.

Sift the flour, salt and baking soda together. Add to the creamed mixture; beat well. Stir in the dates and pecans. Spoon into a greased and floured 5x9-inch loaf pan. Let stand at room temperature for 20 minutes.

Bake at 350 degrees for 50 minutes or until the bread tests done. Cool in the pan for several minutes; remove to a wire rack to cool completely.

yields one loaf

Oatmeal-Applesauce Bread

Ingredients

2	cups bread flour
¼	cup rolled oats
1	tablespoon sugar
1	tablespoon dry milk
1	teaspoon salt
¾	cup water
1	tablespoon butter, softened
¼	cup applesauce
½	teaspoon cinnamon
1	teaspoon fast-rising yeast or 1½ teaspoons dry yeast

Place the flour, oats, sugar, dry milk, salt, water, butter, applesauce and cinnamon in order listed in the loaf pan of a bread machine. Place the yeast in yeast dispenser. Follow bread machine baking instructions for the type of yeast used.

yields one loaf

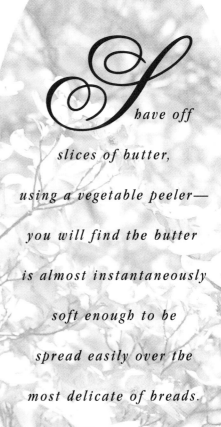

*S*have off slices of butter, using a vegetable peeler— you will find the butter is almost instantaneously soft enough to be spread easily over the most delicate of breads.

Off to

Grandmother's House We Go!

Create a gift for someone

special by baking an assortment

of fresh breads and muffins,

wrapping them in clear plastic

wrap covered by colorful

cellophane and bright ribbons.

Place it all in a decorative

basket and you've got

a great personal gift!

Orange-Glazed Cranberry-Pumpkin Bread

Ingredients

3½	cups flour
1	teaspoon baking powder
2	teaspoons baking soda
2	teaspoons pumpkin pie spice
1½	teaspoons salt
4	eggs
3½	cups sugar
1	cup vegetable oil
1	(16-ounce) can solid-pack pumpkin
2	cups cranberries
1	cup chopped pecans
½	cup confectioners' sugar
2	tablespoons thawed frozen orange juice concentrate
	Dash of allspice

Sift the flour, baking powder, baking soda, pie spice and salt together.

Beat the eggs in a mixer bowl. Add the sugar, oil and pumpkin; beat well. Add the flour mixture gradually, mixing well after each addition. Fold in the cranberries and pecans. Spoon into 2 greased 5x9-inch loaf pans.

Bake at 350 degrees for 55 to 65 minutes or until the bread begins to pull away from sides of the pans. Cool in the pans for 10 minutes; remove to wire racks to cool completely.

Combine the confectioners' sugar and orange juice concentrate in a bowl. Add the allspice and mix well. Drizzle over tops of cooled bread.

yields two loaves

Pepperoni Bread

Ingredients

2	cups bread flour
2	tablespoons sugar
1	tablespoon dry milk
1	teaspoon salt
⅞	cup water
1	tablespoon butter, softened
¼	cup chopped pepperoni
1	teaspoon fast-rising yeast or 1½ teaspoons dry yeast

Place bread flour, sugar, dry milk, salt, water, butter and pepperoni in order listed in the loaf pan of the bread machine. Place the yeast in yeast dispenser. Follow bread machine baking instructions for the type of yeast used.

yields one loaf

Melt-Away Yeast Rolls

Ingredients

1	package dry yeast
2	cups warm water
¾	cup melted margarine
¼	cup sugar
1	large egg
4	cups self-rising flour

Dissolve the yeast in warm water in a large bowl. Add the margarine, sugar and egg; mix well. Add the flour gradually, stirring well after each addition. Drop by spoonfuls into greased muffin cups, filling ⅔ full.

Bake at 425 degrees for 12 to 15 minutes or until brown.

May store dough in refrigerator for 3 to 4 days.

yields twenty-four rolls

Herb Butter:

Blend 1 stick butter with 1½ teaspoons each of fresh tarragon, thyme and oregano with ¼ teaspoon black pepper and 3 tablespoons fresh Italian parsley. Refrigerate in ramekins until firm.

Tints of Spring

First Aid

for Culinary Mishaps:

When bread dough

doesn't rise, set the dough

on a warm heating

pad for a few minutes.

Sour Cream Rolls

Ingredients

1	cup sour cream
1½	packages dry yeast
⅓	cup warm water
1	cup butter, softened
½	cup sugar
½	teaspoon salt
4	cups flour
2	eggs, beaten
¼	cup melted butter

❧ Heat the sour cream in a double boiler over boiling water until slightly yellow around the edge.

❧ Dissolve the yeast in warm water in a bowl. Let stand for 15 minutes.

❧ Combine the butter, sugar and salt in a large bowl. Add the sour cream, stirring until the butter melts. Cool to lukewarm. Stir in 1 cup of the flour. Add the yeast; mix well. Add 1 cup of the remaining flour; beat until smooth. Add eggs and remaining 2 cups flour 1 cup at a time, mixing well after each addition. Chill, covered, in refrigerator for 6 hours to overnight.

❧ Roll out dough on a floured surface; cut into desired shapes. Place on a greased baking sheet; brush tops with melted butter. Let rise, loosely covered, for 1 hour in a warm place.

❧ Bake at 375 degrees for 10 to 15 minutes or until brown.

❧ May keep dough, wrapped in plastic wrap, for several weeks in refrigerator.

yields forty-eight rolls

Best Bread in the World

Ingredients

2	cups boiling water
1	cup rolled oats
2	packages dry yeast
⅓	cup lukewarm water
1	tablespoon salt
½	cup honey
2	tablespoons melted butter
2½	(to 3) cups white bread flour
1½	(to 2) cups whole wheat flour
1	egg yolk, beaten
	Sesame seeds

Pour the boiling water over oats in a large bowl. Let stand until the oats are softened and the mixture is lukewarm.

Dissolve the yeast in lukewarm water in a bowl.

Add the salt, honey and butter to lukewarm oats; mix well. Add yeast; mix well. Add bread flour and whole wheat flour gradually, mixing well after each addition. Knead dough on a lightly floured surface for 10 minutes or until smooth and elastic. Place dough in a greased bowl, turning to coat the surface. Let rise, covered, in a warm place for 1 hour or until doubled in bulk.

Punch dough down; cut into halves. Knead each portion briefly; shape into loaves. Place in 2 greased loaf pans. Let rise, covered, in a warm place until pans are full.

Brush top of each loaf with egg yolk; sprinkle with sesame seeds.

Bake at 350 degrees for 35 to 40 minutes or until the loaves test done. Cool in the pans for several minutes; remove to wire racks to cool completely.

yields two loaves

There is a better way!!! Use a serrated-edge knife that has been heated for ease in cutting freshly baked bread. Another option is to turn bread over on its side to slice, rather than attempting to cut through a hard top crust.

Tints of Spring

Poppy Seed Bread

Ingredients

3	cups flour
1½	teaspoons salt
1½	teaspoons baking powder
1⅛	cups vegetable oil
3	eggs
1½	cups milk
1½	teaspoons almond flavoring
1½	teaspoons vanilla extract
1½	teaspoons butter flavoring
2½	cups sugar
2	tablespoons poppy seeds
½	cup orange juice
¾	cup sugar
½	teaspoon almond flavoring
½	teaspoon vanilla extract
½	teaspoon butter flavoring

Combine the flour, salt, baking powder, oil, eggs, milk, flavorings, 2½ cups sugar and poppy seeds in a mixer bowl; beat at medium speed for 2 minutes. Spoon into 2 greased and floured loaf pans.

Bake at 350 degrees for 1 hour or until the loaves test done.

Combine the orange juice with remaining ¾ cup sugar and flavorings in a saucepan. Bring to a boil, stirring frequently. Pierce holes in warm loaves with a pick; pour the orange glaze over the loaves. Let stand until cool.

yields two loaves

A basket of mixed spring flowers of Iris, snapdragons, tube roses, wax flowers, a few daisies and some pitsporum greenery makes a colorful and casual table decoration.

Swedish Vittebröd

Ingredients

15	cardamom seeds, ground
2	tablespoons butter
¼	cup sugar
1	package Pillsbury Hot Roll Mix
1	egg, beaten
2	tablespoons melted butter
2	teaspoons sugar
1	teaspoon cinnamon

Cardamom seed: A fragrant, cinnamon-like seed used heavily in Swedish baking— whole seeds and ground seeds are used.

❧ Combine the cardamom seeds, 2 tablespoons butter, ¼ cup sugar and the yeast from the roll mix package in a bowl. Add water using package directions, stirring until the yeast is dissolved. Add egg, and mix well. Add the roll mix; blend well.

❧ Knead on a floured surface until smooth and elastic. Place in a greased bowl, turning to grease the surface. Let rise, covered, in a warm place for 1 hour or until doubled in bulk.

❧ Turn out onto a floured surface. Divide dough into 2 portions; divide each portion into 3 portions. Shape each portion into a 12-inch rope. Join 3 ropes together at one end and braid. Place on a greased baking pan. Repeat with remaining ropes. Let rise, covered, in a warm place until doubled in bulk.

❧ Bake at 350 degrees for 30 minutes or until the loaves test done.

❧ Drizzle 2 tablespoons melted butter over loaves; sprinkle with a mixture of 2 teaspoons sugar and cinnamon.

yields two loaves

Tints of Spring

Oatmeal Muffins

Ingredients

1	cup rolled oats
½	cup packed brown sugar
1	cup buttermilk
1	egg
½	cup melted margarine
1	cup sifted flour
2	teaspoons baking powder
1	teaspoon salt
½	teaspoon baking soda

Combine the oats, brown sugar and buttermilk in a bowl. Let stand for 10 minutes or longer. Stir in the egg and margarine. Sift dry ingredients together. Stir into the oat mixture just until mixed. Fill greased muffin cups ¾ full.

Bake at 425 degrees for 15 minutes or until the muffins test done.

yields twelve muffins

Sweet Potato Muffins

Ingredients

¼	cup butter, softened
½	cup sugar
1	egg
1	(16-ounce) can yams, drained
¾	cup flour
2	teaspoons baking powder
½	teaspoon each salt and cinnamon
¼	teaspoon nutmeg
½	cup milk
¼	cup each chopped pecans and raisins

Cream the butter and sugar in a mixer bowl until light and fluffy. Beat in the egg. Add the yams; mix well. Add sifted dry ingredients alternately with milk, mixing just until blended. Stir in the pecans and raisins. Fill the greased muffin cups completely full.

Bake at 400 degrees for 25 minutes or until the muffins test done.

yields thirty-six muffins

Corn Bread Muffins

Ingredients

1	cup each yellow cornmeal and flour
2	teaspoons baking powder
1	teaspoon each baking soda and sugar
½	teaspoon salt
2	egg whites
1¼	cups plain nonfat yogurt
¼	cup vegetable oil

Combine the first 6 ingredients in a bowl; mix well. Make a well in center of the mixture. Combine the egg whites, yogurt and oil in a bowl. Add to the dry ingredients, mixing just until moistened. Fill muffin cups sprayed with nonstick cooking spray ¾ full.

Bake at 425 degrees for 12 to 14 minutes or until the muffins test done.

yields eighteen muffins

Texas Corn Bread

Ingredients

1	cup yellow cornmeal
½	cup flour
1	teaspoon salt
2	tablespoons sugar
1	tablespoon baking powder
½	teaspoon baking soda
1	egg, beaten
1	cup buttermilk
½	cup milk
¼	cup melted butter

Sift the first 6 ingredients into a bowl. Add mixture of egg, buttermilk, milk and butter; mix just until moistened. Heat a greased 9-inch square baking pan in a 450-degree oven for several minutes. Pour batter into hot pan.

Bake at 450 degrees for 15 to 20 minutes or until golden brown. Cut into squares to serve.

yields nine to twelve squares

When making corn bread, add the liquid in two stages to avoid a lumpy batter, because cornmeal doesn't absorb liquid quickly. For a dark, crisp crust, bake the batter in a preheated, greased cast-iron skillet.

Brunch

Whatever

happened to breakfast?

Somewhere between yesterday and

today, breakfast was lost,

strayed or stolen. Lost, perhaps,

to the urgencies of schedules

and commuter trains and car

pools. Strayed into other forms —

such as brunch and coffees.

—*Wilma Dykeman*
Explorations

Tints of Spring

Chiles Rellenos

Ingredients

1	(4-ounce) can chopped green chiles, drained
½	cup shredded Monterey Jack cheese
½	cup shredded sharp Cheddar cheese
1½	cups cottage cheese
1	tablespoon flour
4	eggs
⅔	cup evaporated milk
½	teaspoon salt
¼	teaspoon lemon pepper
¼	teaspoon garlic salt
2	tomatoes, sliced

Combine the green chiles, Monterey Jack cheese, Cheddar cheese and cottage cheese in a bowl; mix well. Stir in the flour; mix well.

Beat the eggs in a mixer bowl until light and fluffy. Add the evaporated milk, salt, lemon pepper and garlic salt, beating constantly. Stir into the cheese mixture. Spoon into a greased 9x13-inch baking dish.

Bake at 325 degrees for 30 minutes. Remove from the oven. Arrange the sliced tomatoes around the edge of the baking dish.

Bake at 325 degrees for 30 minutes longer.

yields eight servings

Crab and Egg Supreme

Ingredients

2	cups soft crust-trimmed bread cubes
2	cups mayonnaise
1½	cups milk
12	hard-cooked eggs, mashed
⅔	cup chopped onion
½	cup sliced stuffed green olives
1	pound fresh crab meat
1	teaspoon salt
¼	teaspoon pepper
1	cup soft crust-trimmed bread crumbs
1	tablespoon butter
	Paprika

Arrange 2 cups bread cubes in a greased 9x13-inch baking dish.

Beat the mayonnaise and milk in a large mixer bowl. Stir in the eggs, onion, olives, crab meat, salt and pepper. Layer over the bread cubes; top with the bread crumbs; dot with butter. Sprinkle with paprika.

Bake at 350 degrees for 30 minutes.

yields twelve servings

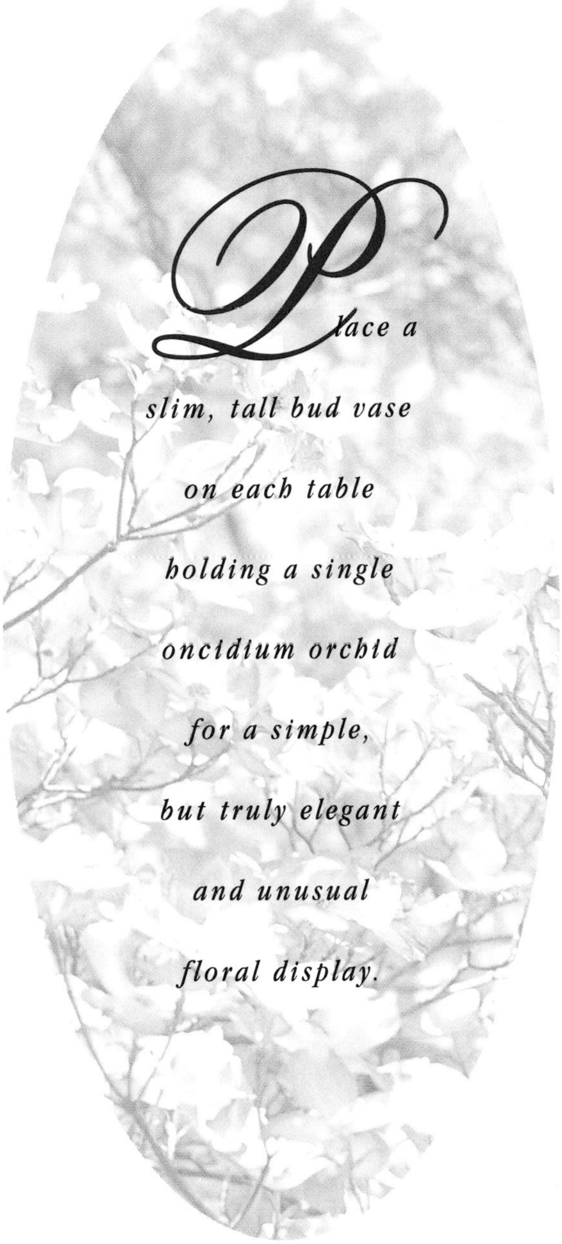

Place a slim, tall bud vase on each table holding a single oncidium orchid for a simple, but truly elegant and unusual floral display.

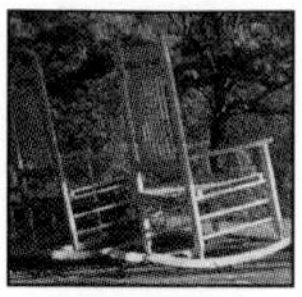

Tints of Spring

Sausage Mushroom Breakfast Casserole

Ingredients

2¼	cups seasoned croutons
1½	pounds hot bulk sausage
4	eggs, beaten
2¼	cups milk
1	(10-ounce) can cream of mushroom soup
1	(4-ounce) can sliced mushrooms, drained
¾	teaspoon dry mustard
2	cups shredded sharp Cheddar cheese

Spread the croutons in a greased 9x13-inch baking dish.

Brown the sausage in a skillet, stirring until crumbly; drain.

Combine the eggs with milk, mushroom soup, mushrooms and mustard in a bowl; mix well.

Layer the sausage and the egg mixture over the croutons. Chill, covered, for 8 hours to overnight in refrigerator. Let stand at room temperature for 30 minutes before baking.

Bake, uncovered, at 325 degrees for 50 to 55 minutes or until bubbly. Sprinkle the cheese over the top.

Bake for 5 minutes longer. Garnish with cherry tomato halves and parsley sprigs.

yields twelve servings

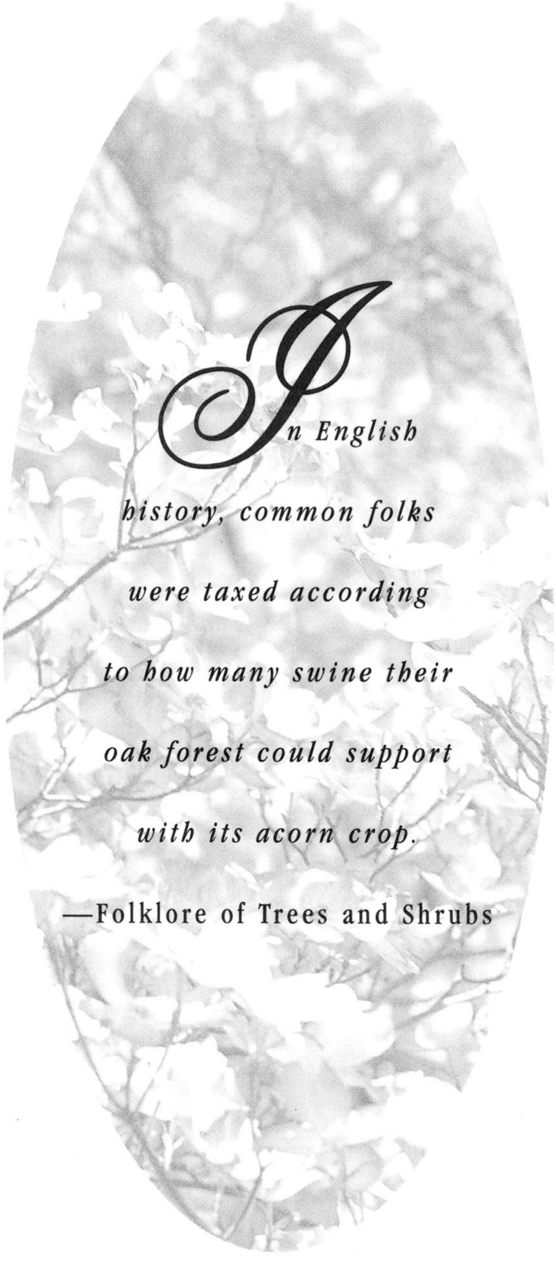

Zucchini and Sausage Quiche

Ingredients

1	(9-inch) unbaked pie shell
2	cups shredded zucchini
¼	cup butter
8	ounces sweet Italian sausage, casing removed
1	cup shredded Swiss cheese
4	eggs
1	cup milk
½	cup whipping cream
¼	cup grated Parmesan cheese
½	teaspoon salt
	Dash of pepper

Bake the pie shell using package directions. Let stand until cool.

Sauté the zucchini in 2 tablespoons of the butter in a large skillet for 5 minutes; drain.

Cook the sausage in the remaining 2 tablespoons butter, stirring until crumbly; drain on paper towels. Layer the zucchini, sausage and Swiss cheese in the cooled pie shell.

Beat the eggs in a mixer bowl. Add the milk, cream, Parmesan cheese, salt and pepper; mix well. Spoon over layers.

Bake at 450 degrees for 15 minutes. Chill in refrigerator. Remove and let stand until 1 hour before serving time or until quiche is of room temperature. Bake at 350 degrees for 30 minutes or until knife inserted near edge comes out clean. Let stand for several minutes before serving.

yields eight servings

Tints of Spring

Pizza for breakfast? Serve this with fresh fruit salad and you've got an easy, make-ahead brunch for friends.

Breakfast Pizza

Ingredients

1	(8-count) can crescent rolls
1	pound bulk pork sausage
1⅓	cups thawed frozen shredded hashed brown potatoes
1½	cups shredded sharp Cheddar cheese
4	large eggs
⅓	cup milk
¾	teaspoon onion salt
¼	teaspoon salt
¼	teaspoon pepper
2	tablespoons Parmesan cheese
2	tablespoons finely chopped green onions

Unroll the crescent roll dough; separate into 2 rectangles. Press onto greased pizza pan, sealing perforations.

Brown the sausage in a skillet, stirring until crumbly; drain. Layer the sausage, potatoes and Cheddar cheese over the dough.

Combine eggs, milk, onion salt, salt and pepper in a mixer bowl; beat well. Pour the mixture over the layers; sprinkle with the Parmesan cheese and green onions.

Bake at 375 degrees for 20 to 25 minutes or until brown. Cut into wedges.

yields eight servings

Grits Soufflé

Ingredients

2   cups uncooked quick-cooking grits

½   cup butter

12   egg yolks, beaten

16   ounces sharp Cheddar cheese, shredded

1   teaspoon salt

12   egg whites, stiffly beaten

    Paprika to taste

Cook the grits using package directions, omitting salt. Stir in the butter until melted. Add the egg yolks, cheese and salt; beat well. Fold in the stiffly beaten egg whites. Spoon into a greased 3-quart baking dish; sprinkle with paprika.

Bake at 350 degrees for 45 minutes or until set.

yields twelve servings

Tomato Pie

Ingredients

1   (9-inch) unbaked pie shell

5   medium tomatoes, cut into ½-inch slices

    Salt and pepper to taste

½   cup chopped fresh basil

⅔   cup shredded sharp Cheddar cheese

⅓   cup mayonnaise

Bake pie shell at 450 degrees for 5 minutes. Let cool.

Arrange the tomato slices in overlapping concentric circles in the pie shell. Add salt, pepper and ½ of the basil. Layer the cheese and mayonnaise over the basil, spreading to the edge of the pie shell. Sprinkle with salt, pepper and the remaining basil.

Bake at 450 degrees for 45 to 50 minutes or until brown and bubbly. Let stand at room temperature for 10 minutes before serving.

yields six servings

What are grits, anyway? Hominy is what is left when white corn kernels are skinned. Hominy grits are ground hominy and are available either coarse, medium or fine— like cornmeal.

Tints of Spring

*F*ruited breads originated because this was the best way to make use of overly ripe fruit.

Banana Brunch Bread

Ingredients

½	cup butter, softened
1	cup sugar
2	eggs
1	cup mashed bananas
½	teaspoon vanilla extract
½	cup sour cream
2	cups sifted flour
1	teaspoon baking powder
¼	teaspoon salt
1	teaspoon baking soda
½	cup chopped pecans
½	cup sugar
½	teaspoon cinnamon
8	ounces whipped cream cheese

Cream the butter and 1 cup sugar in a mixer bowl until light and fluffy. Add the eggs 1 at a time, beating well after each addition.

Combine the bananas, vanilla and sour cream in a bowl; mix well.

Sift the flour, baking powder, salt and baking soda together. Stir the banana mixture and flour mixture into the creamed mixture just until moistened.

Combine the pecans, ½ cup sugar and cinnamon in a bowl; mix well. Sprinkle equal portions of half the mixture into 3 greased 3x7-inch loaf pans. Spoon the batter into the pans; top with the remaining pecan mixture.

Bake at 350 degrees for 45 minutes. Serve with whipped cream cheese.

yields three small loaves

Rise-and-Shine Coffee Cakes

Ingredients

½   cup margarine, softened

1   cup flour

1   tablespoon water

½   cup butter

1   cup water

1   cup flour

3   eggs

1   teaspoon vanilla extract

2   tablespoons butter, softened

1½   cups confectioners' sugar

2   tablespoons hot water

½   teaspoon vanilla extract

     Pinch of salt

Combine ½ cup margarine, 1 cup flour and 1 tablespoon water in a bowl. Stir until the mixture is crumbly. Divide the dough into 2 equal portions. Press 1 portion onto a greased baking sheet.

Press the other portion onto another baking sheet.

Combine ½ cup butter and 1 cup water in a saucepan. Bring to a boil. Pour the mixture into a large mixer bowl. Add 1 cup flour all at once; mix well. Add the eggs 1 at a time, beating well after each addition. Add 1 teaspoon vanilla; beat for 3 minutes. Divide into 2 equal portions. Spread 1 portion on each of the prepared baking sheets. Chill, covered loosely, in refrigerator for 8 hours or longer.

Bake, uncovered, at 350 degrees for 1 hour or until brown.

Combine the remaining 2 tablespoons butter and confectioners' sugar in a mixer bowl; mix well. Add 2 tablespoons hot water, remaining ½ teaspoon vanilla and salt; mix well. Drizzle over the hot coffee cakes. Serve warm.

yields twelve servings

Tints of Spring

The Legend Of The Dogwood

The dogwood once was as

tall and mighty as the oak

and thus was chosen

to make the cross on which

Jesus Christ was crucified.

The dogwood was so

ashamed of its task

that it begged

Jesus for forgiveness.

In His compassion

for all living

things

Raspberry Cream Cheese Danish

Ingredients

2	cups baking mix
3	ounces cream cheese, softened
¼	cup butter, softened
⅓	cup milk
½	cup raspberry preserves
½	cup sifted confectioners' sugar
½	teaspoon vanilla extract
1	tablespoon milk

Place the baking mix in a bowl. Cut in the cream cheese and butter using a pastry blender until mixture is crumbly. Add ⅓ cup milk; mix well. Knead on waxed paper 8 to 10 times. Roll on waxed paper to an 8x12-inch rectangle. Invert onto a greased 10x15-inch baking pan. Spoon the preserves down the middle third of the pastry lengthwise. Cut strips at 1-inch intervals from outer edge to filling. Fold strips alternately across the filling.

Bake at 425 degrees for 12 to 15 minutes or until brown.

Combine confectioners' sugar, vanilla and 1 tablespoon milk in mixer bowl; beat well. Spread over the warm Danish. Garnish with fresh raspberries.

yields eight servings

Fruit Pizza

Ingredients

¼	cup confectioners' sugar
1	cup flour
½	cup margarine, softened
8	ounces low-fat cream cheese, softened
½	cup sugar
½	teaspoon vanilla extract
2	cups assorted fresh fruit such as strawberries, peaches, pineapple, kiwifruit, blueberries or cherries
1	tablespoon cornstarch
¼	cup sugar
1	teaspoon lemon juice
½	cup apple juice

☙ Combine the confectioners' sugar and flour in a bowl. Cut in the margarine until crumbly. Press the dough onto a pizza pan.

☙ Bake at 350 degrees for 8 to 10 minutes. Let stand until cool.

☙ Combine the cream cheese, ½ cup sugar and vanilla in a bowl; mix well. Spread over the cooled crust.

☙ Peel and slice the fruit. Arrange the fruit in circles over the cream cheese layer, starting in the center and layering toward edge.

☙ Combine the cornstarch with ¼ cup sugar in a bowl. Stir in the lemon juice and apple juice. Drizzle over the fruit. Chill thoroughly in refrigerator.

yields eight servings

Jesus took pity on the dogwood and decreed the tree would be slender and twisted so it would never again be used as a cross. As a reminder the dogwood would bear blossoms in the shape of a cross with the center crown of thorns, and each petal edged with nail prints stained with red.

—Folklore of Trees and Shrubs

Tints of Spring

Apple Bake

Ingredients

⅓	cup water
1	cup sugar
2	tablespoons butter
8	apples
⅓	cup water
1	cup chopped pecans
½	cup packed brown sugar
½	teaspoon cinnamon
1	egg, beaten

Combine ⅓ cup water, sugar and butter in a saucepan. Cook just until the sugar is dissolved, stirring constantly. Remove from the heat.

Remove the apple cores. Spray a 3-quart baking dish with nonstick baking spray. Place ⅓ cup water in the baking dish. Arrange apples in the water.

Mix the pecans, brown sugar and cinnamon in a bowl. Add the egg and mix well. Spoon the mixture into the cored apples. Pour the warm syrup over the tops.

Bake at 350 degrees for 1½ to 2 hours or until the apples are tender.

yields eight servings

Apple Butter

Ingredients

1	(12-ounce) can frozen unsweetened apple juice concentrate
1	pound dried, unsulphured sliced apples
4	teaspoons cinnamon
1½	teaspoons allspice
½	teaspoon cloves

Prepare apple juice using package directions to make 1½ quarts. Combine with the apples, cinnamon, allspice and cloves in a large saucepan.

Simmer over medium heat for 30 minutes, stirring occasionally. Remove from the heat and let stand until cooled slightly. Mix with a hand-held electric blender until smooth. Spoon into hot sterilized jars, leaving ½ inch headspace; seal with 2-piece lids. May store in refrigerator for several months or process in boiling water bath for 10 minutes. Note: Unsulphured sliced apples are available in health food stores.

yields six one-half pints

Hot Fruit Compote

Ingredients

1	(1-pound) package dried pitted prunes
1	(6-ounce) package dried apricots, chopped
1	(13-ounce) can pineapple chunks
1	(16-ounce) can cherry pie filling
¼	cup dry white wine
1½	cups water
⅓	cup slivered almonds

Arrange the prunes, apricots and undrained pineapple in a greased 9x13-inch baking dish.

Combine the pie filling, wine and water in a bowl; mix well. Pour over the fruit and sprinkle with the almonds.

Bake at 350 degrees for 1 to 1½ hours or until thickened and bubbly.

yields twelve servings

*F*irst and last,

it is land—land rich with

the loam of centuries,

land spread thin over knobby

hills, land supporting

majestic virgin forests and

succulent grasses and

abundant crops.

—*Wilma Dykeman*
Tennessee,
A History

Shades of Summer

Salads

Side Dishes

*D*on't

you know people who

live as though life were

one long summer?

Without the fever of youth

or the fret of age, they

seek to stay suspended in

the blissful warmth

between any extremes.

—*Wilma Dykeman*
Explorations

Salads

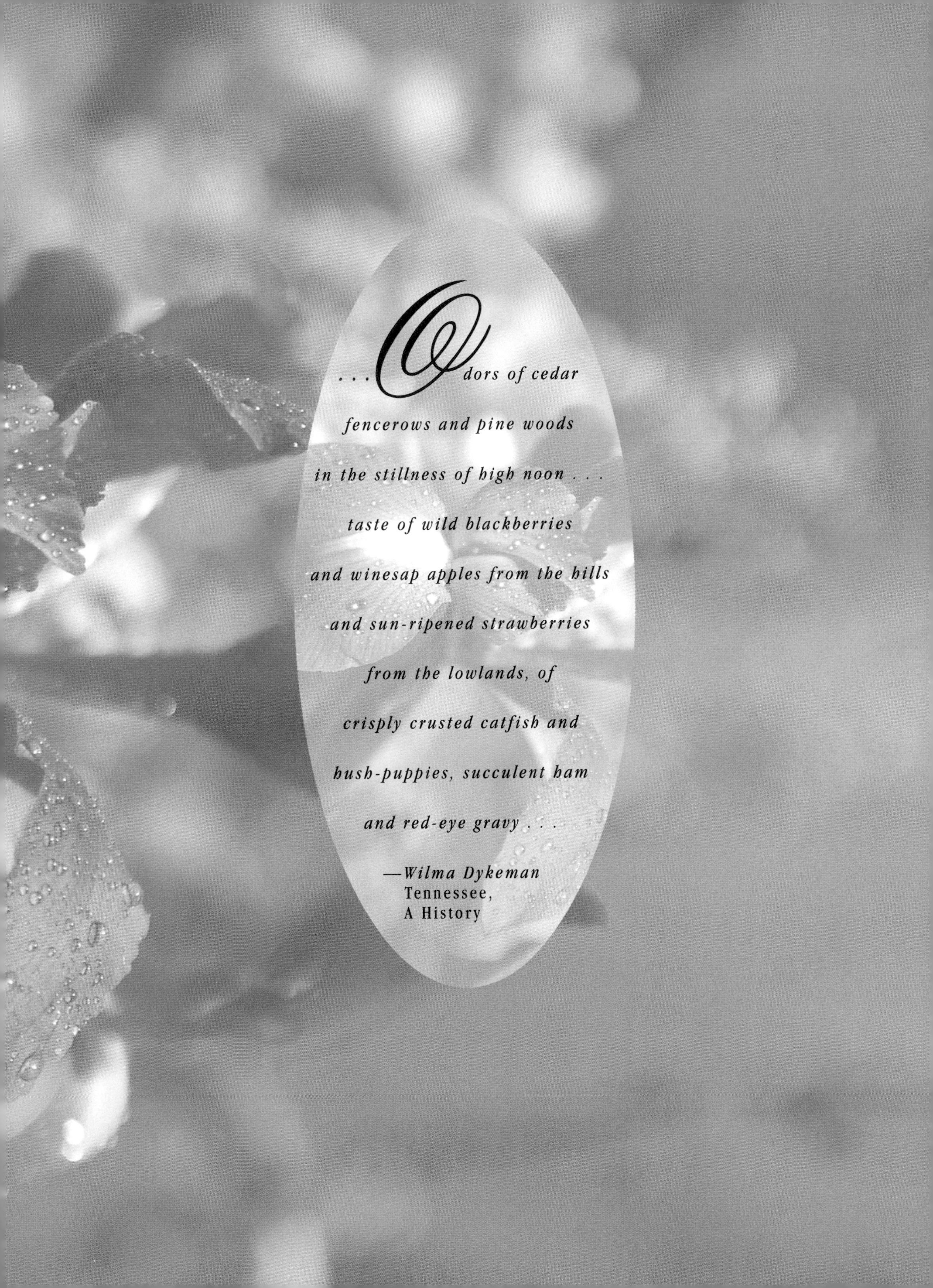

...Odors of cedar

fencerows and pine woods

in the stillness of high noon . . .

taste of wild blackberries

and winesap apples from the hills

and sun-ripened strawberries

from the lowlands, of

crisply crusted catfish and

hush-puppies, succulent ham

and red-eye gravy . . .

—*Wilma Dykeman*
Tennessee,
A History

Shades of Summer

*L*ine

salad plates with

mild flavored mâche or

lemon flavored

sorrel salad greens.

Orange Sherbet Salad

Ingredients

2	(3-ounce) packages orange gelatin
2	cups boiling water
1	pint orange sherbet, softened
1	(8-ounce) can crushed pineapple
1	cup miniature marshmallows
1	(11-ounce) can mandarin oranges, drained
1	cup whipping cream, whipped

Dissolve the gelatin in boiling water in a bowl. Chill until partially set.

Add the orange sherbet, pineapple with juice, marshmallows and mandarin oranges to gelatin; mix well. Fold in the whipped cream. Pour into a mold or 9x13-inch serving dish. Chill until firm.

yields twelve servings

Fruit Salad

Ingredients

1	(20-ounce) can juice-pack pineapple chunks
3	egg yolks
3	tablespoons sugar
2	tablespoons vinegar
1	(17-ounce) can Royal Anne pitted cherries, drained
2	cups miniature marshmallows
3	oranges, peeled, chopped
2	cups whipping cream, whipped

Drain the pineapple, reserving 3 tablespoons pineapple juice. Combine the reserved pineapple juice, egg yolks, sugar and vinegar in a double boiler. Cook over boiling water until thickened, stirring constantly. Let stand until cool.

Combine the pineapple, cherries, marshmallows and oranges in a bowl; toss to mix well.

Fold the whipped cream into the cooled dressing. Pour over the fruit. Chill, covered, for 24 hours.

Serve on a bed of salad greens with a dollop of mayonnaise alongside.

yields eight servings

For easy unmolding of gelatin salads chill the mold and spray it with vegetable spray prior to filling it with the gelatin mixture. You'll find the mold is less likely to hold on to the mixture.

This molded salad makes a delicious summer lunch.

Molded Gazpacho

Ingredients

3	envelopes unflavored gelatin
1	(18-ounce) can tomato juice, chilled
⅓	cup wine vinegar
1	tablespoon salt
	Several drops of Tabasco sauce
2	medium tomatoes, chopped
1	large cucumber, peeled, chopped
1	medium green bell pepper, finely chopped
¼	cup finely chopped onion
1	clove of garlic, minced
1	teaspoon chopped chives
2	large ripe avocados, cut into pieces

Sprinkle the gelatin over ¾ cup of the cold tomato juice in a medium saucepan. Heat over medium heat until gelatin is dissolved, stirring constantly. Remove from the heat. Stir in the remaining tomato juice, vinegar, salt and Tabasco sauce. Cool until the mixture is the texture of egg whites.

Fold in the tomatoes, cucumber, green pepper, onion, garlic, chives and avocados. Pour into an oiled salad mold or individual molds. Chill until set. Garnish with sliced avocado.

yields eight servings

Cold Salmon Mousse with Cucumber Sauce

Ingredients

1	envelope unflavored gelatin
½	cup cold water
3	tablespoons fresh lemon juice
3	tablespoons mayonnaise
¾	teaspoon salt
⅛	teaspoon cayenne
2	cups cold flaked cooked salmon
½	cup whipping cream, whipped
1	cup sour cream
½	cup drained, chopped, seeded cucumber
2	teaspoons chopped chives
¾	teaspoon dillweed
	Salt and freshly ground pepper to taste

The key to great whipped cream: An hour or so before you need to use whipped cream in a recipe, place the beaters and a metallic bowl in the freezer to chill— cream will whip more quickly and peaks will be stiff in no time.

Soften the gelatin in cold water in a saucepan. Heat until the gelatin is dissolved, stirring constantly. Let stand until cool.

Combine the lemon juice, mayonnaise, salt and cayenne in a bowl. Add the cooled gelatin and salmon; mix gently. Fold in the whipped cream. Adjust the seasonings. Pour into an oiled 1-quart mold or individual salad molds. Chill until firm.

Combine the sour cream, cucumber, chives, dillweed, salt and pepper in a bowl. Chill, covered, in refrigerator.

Unmold mousse and serve garnished with cucumber sauce.

yields eight servings

Shades of Summer

A silver Champagne cooler filled with sunflowers and podocarpus greenery is all that is needed for an elegant summer table setting.

Celebration Pasta Salad

Ingredients

1	(16-ounce) package bow tie pasta
	Salt to taste
1	tablespoon extra-virgin olive oil
1	clove of garlic, minced
½	teaspoon salt
½	teaspoon freshly ground pepper
4	teaspoons freshly squeezed lemon juice
2	tablespoons red wine vinegar
½	cup plus 2 tablespoons extra-virgin olive oil
1	teaspoon Italian seasoning
1	yellow bell pepper, chopped
1	red bell pepper, chopped
1	small bunch scallions, chopped
4	ounces prosciutto, finely chopped
½	cup grated Parmesan cheese

Cook the pasta in salted water with 1 tablespoon olive oil in a saucepan using package directions; drain and rinse in cold water.

Combine the garlic, ½ teaspoon salt, pepper, lemon juice, vinegar, ½ cup plus 2 tablespoons olive oil and Italian seasoning in a bowl; mix well.

Combine the pasta, yellow pepper, red pepper, scallions and prosciutto in a large salad bowl. Add the salad dressing; toss to mix. Add the Parmesan cheese; toss to mix.

yields four servings

Greek Orzo Salad

Ingredients

¾	cup uncooked orzo
1	teaspoon olive oil
½	cup plus 2 tablespoons packed fresh dill
1½	cloves of garlic
3	tablespoons olive oil
3	tablespoons fresh lemon juice
1½	tablespoons red wine vinegar
½	teaspoon salt
	Freshly ground pepper to taste
1	pound peeled cooked large shrimp
3½	ounces feta cheese, crumbled
1	large tomato, seeded, chopped
12	kalamata olives, pitted, chopped
2	green onions, sliced

Cook the orzo using package directions; drain. Toss with 1 teaspoon olive oil. Chill in refrigerator.

Place the dill in a food processor container; process until finely chopped. Add the garlic through the feed tube; process until minced. Scrape down the side of container. Add 3 tablespoons olive oil, lemon juice, vinegar, salt and pepper. Process for 5 seconds or until the dressing is blended. Pour into a large bowl.

Add the orzo, shrimp, cheese, tomato, olives and green onions to the dressing; toss gently to mix. Chill, covered, for up to 3 hours before serving.

Serve on lettuce-lined salad plates and garnish with dill sprigs and olives.

yields four servings

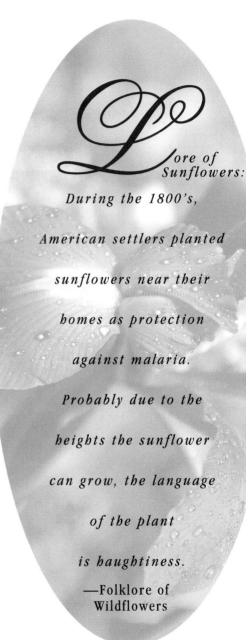

Lore of Sunflowers:

During the 1800's,

American settlers planted

sunflowers near their

homes as protection

against malaria.

Probably due to the

heights the sunflower

can grow, the language

of the plant

is haughtiness.

—Folklore of Wildflowers

Shades of Summer

Barley Salad

Ingredients

3	cups water
1	teaspoon salt
1	cup quick-cooking barley
⅔	cup chopped green bell pepper
⅔	cup chopped red bell pepper
1	(16-ounce) can whole kernel corn, drained
3	tablespoons chopped fresh parsley
¼	cup white wine vinegar
½	cup olive oil
¼	teaspoon salt
¼	teaspoon pepper
⅛	teaspoon paprika

Combine the water, salt and barley in a saucepan. Bring to a boil; reduce heat. Simmer, covered, for 12 to 15 minutes or until the barley is tender, stirring occasionally; drain and cool. Combine the barley, green pepper, red pepper, corn and parsley in a bowl; mix well.

Combine the vinegar, olive oil, salt, pepper and paprika in a bowl; mix well. Pour over the barley mixture, tossing to mix. Chill, covered, for 8 hours or longer.

yields twelve servings

Wild Rice Salad

Ingredients

8	cups water
2	cups wild rice, rinsed
1	green bell pepper, chopped
1	red bell pepper, chopped
1	purple onion, finely chopped
1	(4-ounce) can sliced water chestnuts, drained
1	(4-ounce) can chopped green chiles, drained
1	(4-ounce) can chopped or sliced black olives, drained
½	cup olive oil
3	tablespoons balsamic vinegar
1	teaspoon Dijon mustard
½	teaspoon each salt and pepper

Bring the water to a boil in a large saucepan. Stir in the rice. Simmer, covered, for 1 hour or until the rice is tender. Fluff and cool.

Combine the green pepper, red pepper, onion, water chestnuts, green chiles and olives in a 3-quart bowl.

Combine the oil, vinegar, mustard, salt and pepper in a bowl; mix well. Add the rice to the vegetables; toss to mix. Add the dressing; toss lightly to mix.

yields twelve servings

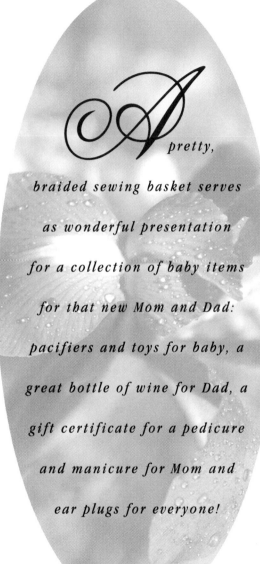

A pretty, braided sewing basket serves as wonderful presentation for a collection of baby items for that new Mom and Dad: pacifiers and toys for baby, a great bottle of wine for Dad, a gift certificate for a pedicure and manicure for Mom and ear plugs for everyone!

Tiny clay

pots filled with

a sunflower

or two (cut short)

provide a

whimsical touch to

an outdoor bar-b-que

display and are easily

transportable!

German Potato Salad

Ingredients

6	(to 8) large new red potatoes
8	(to 16) ounces bacon
2	small onions, chopped
2	(to 3) tablespoons flour
3	(to 4) tablespoons sugar
¼	cup vinegar
¾	cup water
1	cup buttermilk

Boil the unpeeled potatoes with enough water to cover in a saucepan until tender; drain and cool slightly. Peel and slice the potatoes.

Fry the bacon in a skillet until crisp; drain, reserving the bacon drippings. Crumble the bacon.

Sauté the onions in the reserved bacon drippings in the skillet. Stir in the flour and sugar. Cook until thickened, stirring constantly. Stir in the vinegar and ¾ cup water. Add additional water if needed for desired consistency. Remove from the heat. Stir in the buttermilk. Add the potatoes and crumbled bacon, tossing lightly to coat the potatoes with sauce. Spoon into a serving bowl.

yields eight servings

Red Potato Salad

Ingredients

¼	cup red wine vinegar
½	cup vegetable oil
½	teaspoon each garlic salt, onion salt, Good Seasons salad dressing mix and dillweed
1	medium onion, chopped
6	red potatoes, cooked, sliced
4	ounces mozzarella cheese, cut into cubes
2	ounces pepperoni, sliced

Combine the vinegar, oil, garlic salt, onion salt, dressing mix, dillweed and onion in a bowl; mix well. Pour over the potatoes in a large bowl; toss to mix. Add cheese and pepperoni; toss gently. Spoon into a serving bowl.

yields eight servings

Mixed Greens with Bleu Cheese and Raspberry Vinaigrette

Ingredients

8	ounces fresh green beans
16	cups mixed salad greens (Mesclun) such as spinach, romaine, endive, radicchio, Boston lettuce, Bibb lettuce and arugula
½	cup chopped pecans
⅔	cup extra-virgin olive oil
⅔	cup raspberry vinegar
1	clove of garlic, minced
	Salt and freshly ground pepper to taste
1	large cucumber
1	large red bell pepper, cut into strips
1	large yellow bell pepper, cut into strips
5	plum tomatoes, sliced
¾	cup crumbled bleu cheese

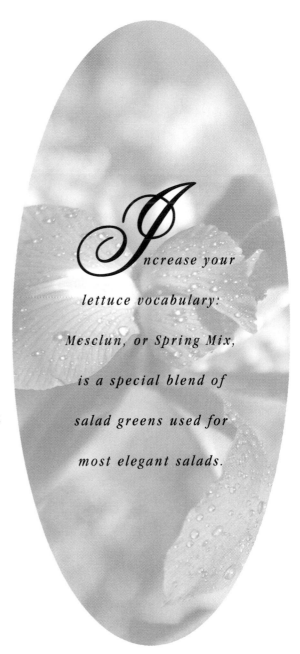

Increase your lettuce vocabulary: Mesclun, or Spring Mix, is a special blend of salad greens used for most elegant salads.

Rinse and trim the green beans; place in a steamer. Steam over boiling water for 2 to 3 minutes or until tender-crisp. Plunge into cold water. Drain and pat dry. Chill, covered, in refrigerator.

Rinse the salad greens; pat dry. Combine and toss in a large bowl. Chill, covered, in refrigerator.

Place pecans in a large baking pan. Bake at 350 degrees for 3 to 5 minutes or until toasted, stirring frequently. Let stand until cool.

Combine the olive oil, vinegar, garlic, salt and pepper in a jar; cover and shake to mix. Let stand at room temperature.

Peel the cucumber; score with a fork vertically. Cut into slices.

Place the salad greens on individual salad plates. Arrange the cucumber, red and yellow peppers, tomatoes and green beans over salad greens. Sprinkle with bleu cheese. Chill until serving time. Sprinkle the salads with toasted pecans. Mix the vinaigrette again; drizzle 2 tablespoons vinaigrette onto each salad.

yields ten servings

Mixed Greens with Warm Roquefort Dressing

Ingredients

16	cups assorted greens such as green leaf lettuce, Boston lettuce, endive, watercress and arugula
¾	cup chopped walnuts
2	tablespoons walnut oil
1	tablespoon vegetable oil
8	ounces Roquefort cheese, crumbled
2	tablespoons sherry vinegar
½	cup whipping cream
¼	teaspoon salt
¼	teaspoon freshly ground pepper
1	Granny Smith apple, cut into ½-inch cubes

Rinse the salad greens; pat dry. Tear into bite-sized pieces. Place in a large bowl; toss to mix. Chill, covered, in refrigerator.

Place the walnuts in a large baking pan. Bake at 350 degrees for 3 to 4 minutes or until toasted, stirring frequently.

Combine the walnut oil, vegetable oil and cheese in a large saucepan. Heat over medium heat until the cheese is melted, whisking constantly. Add the vinegar, cream, salt and pepper. Cook for 10 minutes or until heated through, whisking constantly.

Arrange the salad greens on individual salad plates. Top with toasted walnuts and apple cubes. Drizzle 2 to 3 tablespoons warm dressing on each salad. Serve immediately.

yields twelve servings

Flavored oils and vinegars make traditional salad dressings gourmet-special.

Best-Ever Green Salad

Ingredients

1	cup vegetable oil
⅔	cup sugar
½	teaspoon dry mustard
2	(to 3) teaspoons chopped onion
½	teaspoon garlic salt
	Pepper to taste
⅓	cup vinegar
6	leaves red tip lettuce
6	leaves Boston lettuce
½	(8-ounce) can tiny peas, drained
6	(to 8) slices crisp-cooked bacon, crumbled
4	ounces Swiss cheese, shredded
2	ounces sliced almonds, toasted

Combine the oil, sugar, mustard, onion, garlic salt, pepper and vinegar in a blender container; process until blended.

Tear the lettuce into bite-sized pieces. Combine the lettuce, peas, crumbled bacon, cheese and almonds in a salad bowl. Add ½ of the salad dressing; toss to mix. Chill the remaining salad dressing in a covered container in refrigerator.

yields six servings

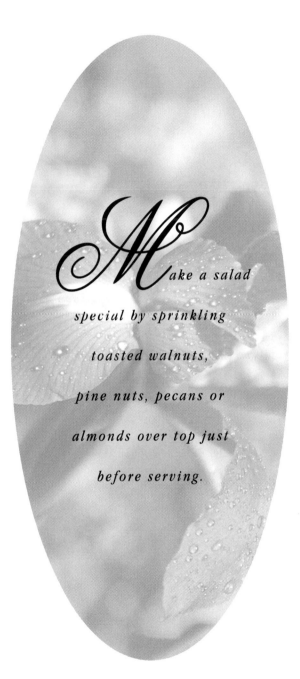

Make a salad special by sprinkling toasted walnuts, pine nuts, pecans or almonds over top just before serving.

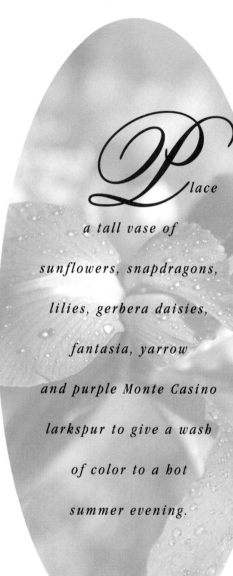

*P*lace

a tall vase of

sunflowers, snapdragons,

lilies, gerbera daisies,

fantasia, yarrow

and purple Monte Casino

larkspur to give a wash

of color to a hot

summer evening.

Brutus Salad

Ingredients

¾	cup olive oil
¼	cup red wine or balsamic vinegar
6	anchovy fillets, minced
4	teaspoons minced garlic
1	tablespoon lemon juice
1	tablespoon Dijon mustard
1	teaspoon white pepper
1	cup (or more) freshly grated Parmesan cheese
1	large head romaine, torn into bite-sized pieces
1½	(to 2) cups croutons

Blend the oil, vinegar, anchovies, garlic, lemon juice, mustard and pepper in a food processor. Add 1 cup cheese; process until blended.

Toss the romaine with desired amount of dressing and croutons in a salad bowl until well coated. Spoon onto individual salad plates. May top with additional croutons and Parmesan cheese.

yields six servings

Caesar Croutons

Ingredients

3	tablespoons butter
3	tablespoons olive oil
3	cups ½-inch cubes of dried bread
2	large cloves of garlic, minced
1	teaspoon chopped fresh parsley
1	teaspoon chopped fresh chives
1	teaspoon chopped fresh tarragon
3	tablespoons freshly grated Parmesan cheese

Heat the butter and olive oil in a large skillet over medium-high heat, stirring until blended. Add the bread cubes, tossing to coat well. Reduce heat to medium-low. Add the garlic, parsley, chives and tarragon, tossing to coat bread cubes. Cook for 20 minutes or until bread cubes are brown, tossing frequently.

Spoon into a large bowl; add Parmesan cheese, tossing to coat. Spread on a flat surface to cool to room temperature. Store in an airtight container.

yields three cups

Roasted Garlic Caesar Salad

Ingredients

2	large heads of garlic
¼	cup dry vermouth
1	tablespoon olive oil
	Pepper to taste
1	tablespoon red wine vinegar
2	tablespoons fresh lemon juice
1	teaspoon Dijon mustard
1	tablespoon anchovy paste
1	teaspoon Worcestershire sauce
	Dash of Tabasco sauce
⅓	cup olive oil
2	large heads romaine
1¼	cups grated Parmesan cheese
3	cups Caesar Croutons (see page 72)

op with large grilled shrimp, slices of grilled chicken or tenderloin for a healthy summer lunch or dinner.

✂ Peel off the papery outer skin of whole garlic, leaving heads intact; place in a small baking dish. Pour the vermouth over garlic. Drizzle with 1 tablespoon olive oil. Season with pepper. Bake, covered with foil, at 300 degrees for 1½ hours or until the garlic is very soft like paste. Let stand until cool. Squeeze garlic to remove cloves from skins; place in a small bowl. Mash with a fork to form paste; place in a blender container. Add the vinegar, lemon juice, mustard, anchovy paste, Worcestershire sauce and Tabasco sauce. Add ⅓ cup olive oil in a fine stream, processing constantly until smooth. May prepare up to 2 hours before serving. Let stand at room temperature.

✂ Tear the romaine into bite-sized pieces; place in a salad bowl. Pour in the dressing, tossing to mix. Add the cheese and croutons; toss to mix. Season with pepper. Serve immediately.

yields eight servings

Spinach and Apple Salad

Ingredients

¼	cup vegetable oil
3	tablespoons red wine vinegar
1	teaspoon sugar
½	teaspoon prepared mustard
	Salt and freshly ground pepper to taste
5	slices bacon
¼	cup sliced almonds
8	cups spinach, rinsed, drained, torn into bite-sized pieces
1	Red Delicious apple, cored, chopped
3	green onions, sliced

Combine the oil, vinegar, sugar, mustard, salt and pepper in a bowl; mix well. Chill, covered, in refrigerator.

Fry the bacon until crisp in a skillet; drain, reserving 1 tablespoon bacon drippings. Crumble the bacon.

Sauté the almonds in 1 tablespoon bacon drippings in a skillet until brown; drain and cool.

Combine the spinach, apple, green onions, sautéed almonds and crumbled bacon in a salad bowl. Add the dressing, tossing gently to mix.

yields eight servings

Strawberry-Spinach Salad

Ingredients

1	pound fresh spinach
¾	cup slivered almonds
2	tablespoons butter
½	cup sugar
2	tablespoons sesame seeds
¼	teaspoon paprika
½	cup vegetable oil
1	tablespoon poppy seeds
1½	teaspoons minced onion
¼	cup cider vinegar
¼	cup white wine vinegar
1	pint fresh strawberries, sliced

Rinse the spinach leaves; pat dry with paper towels. Tear into bite-sized pieces; place in a salad bowl. Chill, covered, in refrigerator.

Sauté the almonds in butter in a skillet until brown; drain and cool.

Combine the sugar, sesame seeds, paprika, oil, poppy seeds, onion, cider vinegar and wine vinegar in a bowl; mix well.

Add the strawberries and almonds to the spinach; toss to mix. Pour in the dressing; toss to mix. Serve immediately.

yields six servings

Fill sink with fresh, cold water and let fresh spinach leaves soak to remove sand particles and dirt; drain. You may need to repeat a few times to be sure leaves are cleaned well and sediment is gone.

Shades of Summer

Poppy Seed Salad Dressing

Ingredients

¾	cup sugar
1	teaspoon dry mustard
1	teaspoon salt
⅓	cup red wine vinegar
1¼	teaspoons onion juice
1	cup vegetable oil
1½	tablespoons poppy seeds

Combine the sugar, mustard, salt, vinegar and onion juice in a blender container. Add the oil in a fine stream, processing constantly until smooth. Stir in the poppy seeds. Chill, covered, in refrigerator for 8 to 12 hours.

Serve over fresh fruit.

yields two cups

Honey Dijon Salad Dressing

Ingredients

1	cup mayonnaise
¼	cup Dijon mustard
¼	cup honey
¾	teaspoon cider vinegar
⅛	teaspoon onion powder
	Dash of red pepper
¼	cup vegetable oil

Combine the mayonnaise, mustard, honey, vinegar, onion powder and red pepper in a blender container. Add the oil in a fine stream, processing constantly until smooth.

May store, covered, in refrigerator for 2 weeks.

yields one and three-fourth cups

Southern Cole Slaw Dressing

Ingredients

1	(7-ounce) bottle chili sauce
¾	cup vegetable oil
½	cup sugar
½	cup water
¾	cup mayonnaise
1	tablespoon Worcestershire sauce
1	teaspoon tarragon
1	onion, finely chopped
½	lemon
	Dash of paprika

Combine the chili sauce, oil, sugar, water, mayonnaise, Worcestershire sauce, tarragon, onion, lemon and paprika in a blender container; process until smooth.

May store, tightly covered, in refrigerator for 2 weeks.

yields one and one-half quarts

Tarragon Vinaigrette

Ingredients

½	cup vegetable oil
¼	cup tarragon wine vinegar
¼	cup sugar
½	teaspoon salt
¼	teaspoon pepper
¼	teaspoon (or more) hot sauce

Combine the oil, vinegar, sugar, salt, pepper and hot sauce in a jar. Cover tightly; shake to mix. Chill, covered, in refrigerator.

If using a metal cover, place waxed paper over jar before adding cover.

yields one cup

Make your own herb vinegar by decanting wine vinegar into sterilized jars filled with several sprigs of your favorite herb. Store in a cool, dark place for several weeks. Strain into pretty jars with a sprig of fresh herb.

Side Dishes

Asparagus and Artichokes

Carrots with Shiitake Mushrooms and
Rosemary-Madeira Sauce

Kahlúa Glazed Carrots

Eggplant with Basil

Mushrooms au Gratin

Parmesan Potatoes

Potato Gratiné

Spinach and Artichoke Casserole

Sweet Potato Casserole

Summer Vegetable Medley

Vegetable Mornay

Garden Medley

Neapolitan Tomato Sauce for Pasta

Rice with Pine Nuts

Marinated Tomatoes

Sauce and Topping for Green Vegetables

Pesto

. . . Touch of

fresh wind ushering rain-

clouds after a long drought over

scalded strips of interstate

highways and parched hay fields,

feel of emerald woods-moss

velvety against the hand, and

knife-sharp blades of dried corn

fodder, prick of late-

summer Spanish needles, . . .

—Wilma Dykeman
Tennessee,
A History

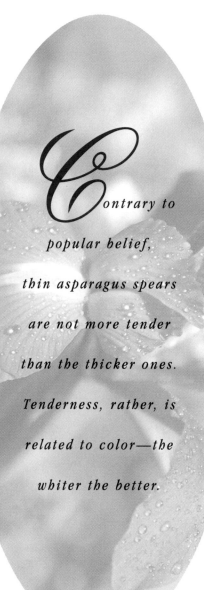

Contrary to popular belief, thin asparagus spears are not more tender than the thicker ones. Tenderness, rather, is related to color—the whiter the better.

Asparagus and Artichokes

Ingredients

1	cup vegetable oil
½	cup tarragon vinegar
2	teaspoons salt
½	teaspoon paprika
2	tablespoons chopped onion
2	tablespoons chopped fresh parsley
2	tablespoons grated lemon rind
½	teaspoon sugar
1	teaspoon Worcestershire sauce
2	pounds fresh asparagus, trimmed
2	(16-ounce) cans artichoke hearts

Combine the oil, vinegar, salt, paprika, onion, parsley, lemon rind, sugar and Worcestershire sauce in a saucepan. Cook over low heat until heated through.

Cook the asparagus in a steamer for several minutes or just until tender - crisp. Arrange asparagus spears in 1 row in center of 4-quart casserole, alternating tops.

Cut the artichoke hearts into halves. Arrange around the asparagus. Pour heated mixture over the top.

Bake, covered with foil, at 350 degrees for 20 minutes.

yields fourteen servings

Carrots with Shiitake Mushrooms and Rosemary-Madeira Sauce

Ingredients

2	cloves of garlic, minced
2	(to 3) tablespoons olive oil
1	pound carrots, sliced
8	ounces shiitake mushrooms, sliced
1½	teaspoons chopped fresh rosemary
1½	cups madeira
½	cup chicken bouillon or stock
	Salt and pepper to taste

Sauté the garlic in olive oil in a large skillet over medium-high heat until soft. Add the carrots. Cook until slightly brown. Add the mushrooms. Cook until tender. Stir in the rosemary, wine and bouillon.

Bring to a boil. Reduce heat to low. Simmer until the liquid has been absorbed and the carrots are tender. Add salt and pepper.

yields four servings

Arrange mixed flowers with a few daisies and a combination of greenery in a pretty basket for a fresh springtime look.

A pottery

pitcher filled with

sunflowers and

Bells of Ireland is great

and easy to do for

a family picnic outing.

Kahlúa Glazed Carrots

Ingredients

3	cups diagonally sliced carrots
1	tablespoon butter
1	tablespoon brown sugar
1	tablespoon honey
3	tablespoons Kahlúa
1	teaspoon cornstarch

Cook the carrots in a steamer for 4 to 5 minutes or until just tender-crisp.

Melt the butter in a large skillet over medium heat. Stir in the brown sugar, honey and 2 tablespoons of the Kahlúa. Cook over medium heat until bubbly, stirring constantly.

Mix the remaining 1 tablespoon Kahlúa with cornstarch in a bowl. Stir into the brown sugar mixture. Cook until thickened, stirring constantly. Add the carrots, tossing to coat with the glaze. Cook until heated through.

yields six servings

Eggplant with Basil

Ingredients

12	(¼-inch) eggplant slices
12	(¼-inch) tomato slices
	Olive oil for frying
	Salt and pepper to taste
12	slices mozzarella cheese
6	tablespoons chopped fresh basil
2	tablespoons olive oil

Fry the eggplant and tomatoes in olive oil in an electric skillet at 325 degrees, adding additional olive oil as needed.

Remove the eggplant to a hot serving platter; top with the tomatoes. Sprinkle with salt and pepper. Top with cheese slices; sprinkle with basil.

Heat the 2 tablespoons olive oil in a skillet; drizzle over the layers. Serve hot.

yields six servings

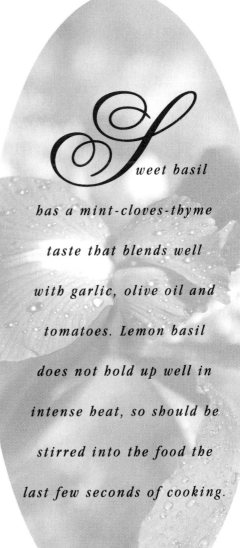

Sweet basil has a mint-cloves-thyme taste that blends well with garlic, olive oil and tomatoes. Lemon basil does not hold up well in intense heat, so should be stirred into the food the last few seconds of cooking.

Mushrooms au Gratin

Ingredients

2	pounds fresh mushrooms, sliced
¼	cup butter
⅔	cup sour cream
2	tablespoons flour
½	teaspoon salt
½	teaspoon pepper
½	cup chopped fresh parsley
1	cup shredded Swiss cheese

Sauté the mushrooms in butter in a skillet for 1 minute. Cook, covered, over low heat for about 5 minutes or until the liquid is extracted from the mushrooms.

Mix the sour cream, flour, salt and pepper in a bowl. Stir into the mushrooms. Bring to a boil. Remove from the heat. Pour into an ungreased 8x12-inch casserole.

Combine the parsley and Swiss cheese in a bowl. Sprinkle over the mushrooms.

Bake at 425 degrees for 10 minutes. May be made ahead and chilled in the refrigerator until baking time.

yields eight servings

Parmesan Potatoes

Ingredients

¾	cup freshly grated Parmesan cheese
1	teaspoon Praise Allah seasoning
½	teaspoon seasoning salt
⅛	teaspoon pepper
4	baking potatoes, unpeeled, cut into slices
¼	cup melted butter
8	ounces bacon, crisp-cooked, crumbled
1½	cups shredded Cheddar cheese

Combine the Parmesan cheese, seasoning, seasoning salt and pepper in a shallow bowl; mix well. Dip the potato slices into the mixture, coating both sides. Place in a 9x13-inch baking dish sprayed with nonstick cooking spray. Sprinkle with any remaining Parmesan cheese mixture; drizzle with melted butter.

Bake at 425 degrees for 30 minutes. Sprinkle with crumbled bacon and Cheddar cheese. Bake for 5 minutes longer.

Serve with catsup or sour cream.

yields four servings

A great accompaniment for hamburgers, turkeyburgers, veggieburgers . . . whichever burger you prefer!

Pronounced

"bour-senh" . . . . this is

a wonderfully flavorful herbed

cheese that livens up

just about any entrée. Alouette

cheese with herbs and

garlic may be substituted

if necessary.

Potato Gratiné

Ingredients

2   cups whipping cream

1   (5-ounce) package boursin cheese with herbs

3   pounds red new potatoes, unpeeled, thinly sliced

      Salt and pepper to taste

1½   tablespoons chopped fresh parsley

Combine the whipping cream and cheese in a large heavy saucepan. Cook over medium heat until the cheese is melted, stirring frequently.

Arrange half the potatoes in a buttered 9x13-inch baking dish, slightly overlapping edges. Sprinkle with salt and pepper and spoon half the cheese sauce over the top. Repeat layers with the remaining ingredients.

Bake at 400 degrees for 1 hour or until the potatoes are tender when pierced with fork and the top is golden brown. Sprinkle with parsley.

yields eight servings

Spinach and Artichoke Casserole

Ingredients

2	cloves of garlic, minced
1	bunch scallions, minced
¼	cup olive oil
8	ounces fresh mushrooms, sliced
2	(10-ounce) packages frozen chopped spinach, thawed, drained
2	(16-ounce) cans artichoke hearts, drained
2½	tablespoons flour
1	cup half-and-half
½	teaspoon nutmeg
1	tablespoon fresh lemon juice
	Salt and pepper to taste
1	cup nonfat sour cream
½	cup Parmesan cheese
	Paprika to taste

Sauté the garlic and scallions in olive oil in a large skillet until tender. Add the mushrooms. Sauté for 5 minutes. Add the spinach and half the artichoke hearts. Cook for 3 minutes. Stir in the flour gradually. Cook for 1 to 2 minutes, stirring constantly. Stir in the half-and-half gradually. Cook until thickened, stirring constantly. Stir in the nutmeg, lemon juice, salt and pepper; mix well. Spoon into a greased 9x13-inch baking dish. Arrange remaining artichoke hearts on top.

Mix the sour cream, Parmesan cheese and paprika in a bowl. Spread over the artichoke hearts.

Bake at 350 degrees for 40 minutes. Serve hot.

yields twelve servings

Use fresh sweet potatoes for the best flavor.

Sweet Potato Casserole

Ingredients

3	cups mashed cooked sweet potatoes
½	cup sugar
¼	cup butter, softened
½	cup evaporated milk
¼	teaspoon salt
¾	cup packed light brown sugar
¼	cup flour
¼	cup butter, softened
1	cup chopped pecans

Combine the sweet potatoes, sugar, ¼ cup butter, evaporated milk and salt in a mixer bowl; mix well. Spoon into a buttered 1½-quart casserole.

Combine the brown sugar, flour and remaining ¼ cup butter in a bowl; mix well. Stir in the pecans. Sprinkle topping over the casserole.

Bake at 350 degrees for 45 minutes.

yields eight servings

Summer Vegetable Medley

Ingredients

2	tablespoons vegetable oil
4	medium yellow squash, sliced
2	medium green bell peppers, cut into strips
1	large onion, cut into rings
8	ounces fresh mushrooms, sliced
1	large clove of garlic, minced
1	teaspoon basil
½	teaspoon salt
½	teaspoon pepper
½	cup chablis or other dry white wine
1	tablespoon butter
½	cup grated Parmesan cheese

Heat the oil in a large skillet. Add the squash, green peppers, onion rings, mushrooms, garlic, basil, salt and pepper. Cook, covered, for 5 minutes. Add the wine.

Simmer, uncovered, for 10 minutes, stirring gently occasionally. Stir in the butter until melted. Spoon into a serving dish. Sprinkle with Parmesan cheese.

yields six servings

Great side dish with ham or roast beef.

Vegetable Mornay

Ingredients

2	tablespoons margarine
1	cup sliced yellow squash
1	cup cauliflowerets
1	cup broccoli florets
¼	teaspoon garlic salt
¼	cup margarine
¼	cup flour
2	cups half-and-half
	Dash of nutmeg
¼	cup Parmesan cheese
1	teaspoon salt
¼	teaspoon thyme
¼	teaspoon garlic salt
2	tablespoons sherry
2	cups soft bread cubes
¼	cup melted margarine
	Paprika to taste

Heat 2 tablespoons margarine in a large skillet. Add the squash, cauliflowerets and broccoli. Sprinkle with ¼ teaspoon garlic salt. Stir-fry vegetables just until tender-crisp; drain.

Combine ¼ cup margarine and flour in a saucepan. Cook over low heat. Stir in the half-and-half, nutmeg, Parmesan cheese, salt, thyme, ¼ teaspoon garlic salt and sherry. Cook over low heat until thickened, stirring constantly. Remove from heat. Add vegetables, tossing gently to coat vegetables. Spoon into a buttered 9x13-inch baking dish. Sprinkle with bread cubes; drizzle with melted margarine. Sprinkle with paprika.

Bake at 350 degrees for 30 minutes or until brown and bubbly.

yields eight servings

Garden Medley

Ingredients

1	large onion, chopped
1	clove of garlic, minced
2	tablespoons olive oil
2	large tomatoes, coarsely chopped
2	medium zucchini, cut into ½-inch slices
2	yellow squash, cut into ½-inch slices
1	tablespoon chopped fresh basil
1	teaspoon fresh chopped parsley
1	cup shredded mozzarella cheese

Sauté the onion and garlic in olive oil in a large skillet. Add tomatoes, zucchini and yellow squash. Stir-fry just until the vegetables are tender-crisp. Stir in the basil and parsley.

Spoon into a warm serving dish. Top with the cheese.

yields ten servings

Neapolitan Tomato Sauce for Pasta

Ingredients

1	(to 1½) pounds tomatoes, peeled, seeded, chopped
1	clove of garlic, minced
¼	teaspoon sugar
	Salt and freshly ground pepper to taste
3	tablespoons olive oil
1	tablespoon finely chopped fresh basil
12	ounces spaghetti

Combine the tomatoes, garlic, sugar, salt, pepper and olive oil in a large saucepan. Cook over medium heat for 20 minutes, stirring occasionally. Stir in the basil. Adjust the seasonings.

Cook the spaghetti using package directions; drain. Add spaghetti to the tomato sauce, tossing gently to coat. Spoon into a serving dish.

yields four servings

Rice with Pine Nuts

Ingredients

¼	cup pine nuts
3	tablespoons minced onion
1	clove of garlic, minced
2½	tablespoons butter
1	cup uncooked rice
1½	cups chicken broth
2	sprigs of parsley
¼	teaspoon thyme
½	bay leaf
⅛	teaspoon cayenne

Place the pine nuts in a large baking pan. Bake at 325 degrees for 10 minutes or until toasted, stirring after 5 minutes.

Sauté the onion and garlic in butter in a large skillet until tender. Stir in the rice. Add the chicken broth and mix well. Stir in the parsley, thyme, bay leaf and cayenne.

Bring to a boil; reduce heat to low. Simmer, covered, for 20 to 25 minutes or until the broth has been absorbed. Remove the ½ bay leaf. Stir in the pine nuts. Spoon into a serving dish.

yields four servings

Marinated Tomatoes

Ingredients

6	tomatoes
⅓	cup vegetable oil
¼	cup red wine vinegar
1	clove of garlic, minced
¼	cup finely chopped parsley
¼	cup finely chopped green onions and tops
1	teaspoon salt
¼	teaspoon freshly cracked pepper
½	teaspoon thyme

Immerse the tomatoes briefly in boiling water in a saucepan. Rinse with cold water and remove peel. Slice the tomatoes thinly and arrange in a shallow dish.

Combine the oil, vinegar, garlic, parsley, green onions, salt, pepper and thyme in a large bowl; mix well. Pour over the tomatoes.

Marinate, covered, in refrigerator for several hours before serving.

yields six to eight servings

Serve with thick-crust, fresh French bread, slices of cheese and a salad . . . you've got a light summer meal.

Sauce and Topping for Green Vegetables

Ingredients

2	ounces sharp Cheddar cheese, grated
¼	cup milk
1	egg, beaten
¼	cup mayonnaise
¼	cup bread crumbs
1	tablespoon melted butter

❧ Combine the cheese, milk, egg and mayonnaise in a bowl; mix well. Toss gently with cooked vegetable of your choice such as broccoli, green beans or cabbage. Spoon vegetables into a casserole. Mix the bread crumbs and butter in a bowl. Sprinkle over the vegetables.

❧ Bake at 350 degrees for 30 to 35 minutes or until brown.

yields 2 cups sauce

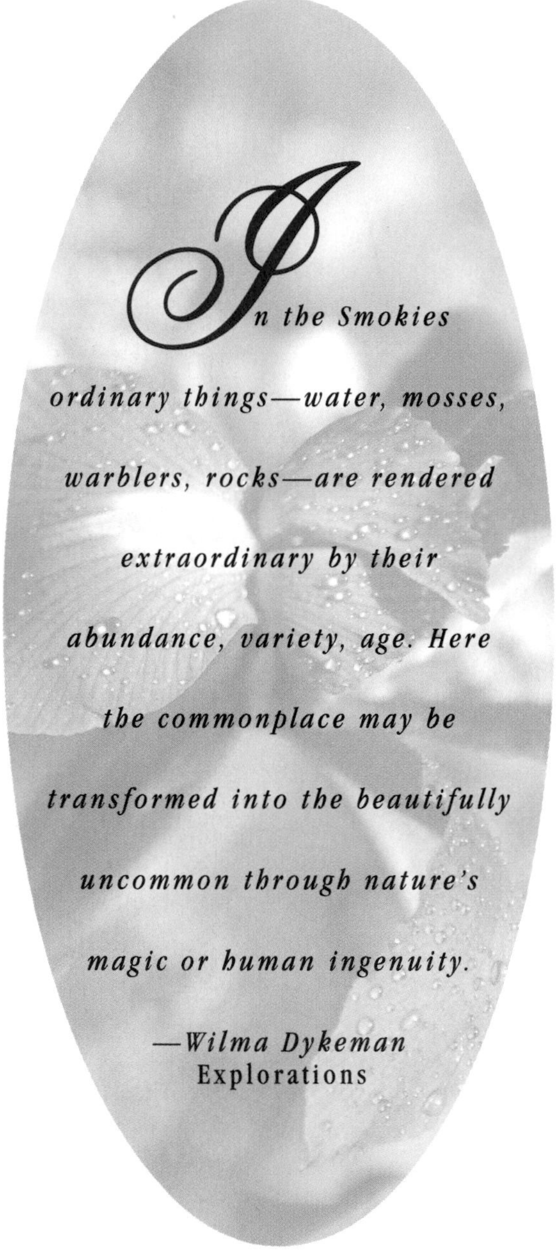

*I*n the Smokies ordinary things—water, mosses, warblers, rocks—are rendered extraordinary by their abundance, variety, age. Here the commonplace may be transformed into the beautifully uncommon through nature's magic or human ingenuity.

—*Wilma Dykeman*
Explorations

Pesto

Ingredients

1	cup packed fresh basil leaves
⅓	cup pine nuts
⅓	cup grated Parmesan cheese
⅓	cup olive oil
¼	teaspoon salt
1	clove of garlic, minced
8	ounces uncooked pasta

❧ Combine the basil leaves, pine nuts, Parmesan cheese, olive oil, salt and garlic in a food processor container; process until puréed.

❧ Cook the pasta using package directions; drain. Spoon into a serving bowl; toss with the pesto.

yields six servings

Not just for pasta, pesto can be added to dips, sour cream for baked potatoes, salad dressings or cream soups.

Harvest Hues

ENTRÉES

SOUPS

TAILGATING

*R*ecollection

of my own first visit to the

Smokies is as wrapped

in haze as Clingmans Dome

on a rainy autumn morning....

Southern Appalachia's

deciduous hardwood forests

were in brilliant color.

—*Wilma Dykeman*
Explorations

Entrées

Beef in Burgundy

Three-Day Brisket

Bourbon Filets

Veal Scaloppine

Grilled Butterflied
Leg of Lamb with Herbs

Marinated London Broil

Madeira Sauce

Barbecue Sauce

Grilled Pork Tenderloin

Chinese Pork Tenderloin

Baked Stuffed Pork
Tenderloin

Stuffed Pizza

Boursin-Stuffed
Chicken Breasts

Peppered Chicken Breasts
with Rosemary and Garlic

Sherried Chicken Breasts

Vermouth-Poached
Chicken with Rice

Chicken Marsala

Chicken Pot Pie

Chicken Enchiladas

Texas-Style Cornish
Game Hens

Elegant Orange Roughy

Marinated Grilled Tuna

Maryland Crab Cakes with
Herb Mayonnaise

Lobster Linguini in
Tomato Cream Sauce

Cajun Seafood Carbonara

Sea Scallops Florentine

Shrimp Thermidor

Ocean Spring Shrimp

Mustard Mint Sauce

Lemon-Chive Topping

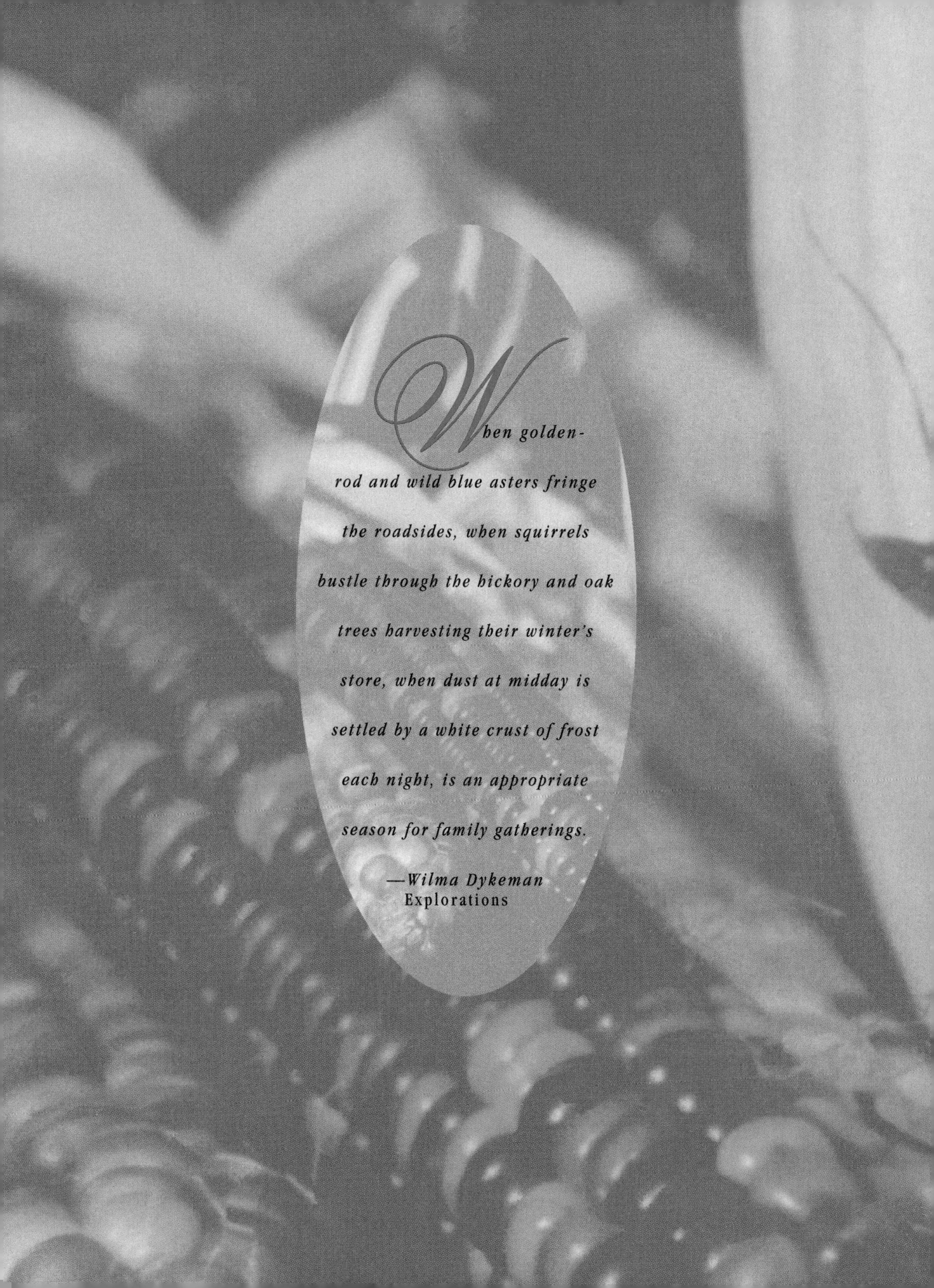

*W*hen golden-
rod and wild blue asters fringe

the roadsides, when squirrels

bustle through the hickory and oak

trees harvesting their winter's

store, when dust at midday is

settled by a white crust of frost

each night, is an appropriate

season for family gatherings.

—*Wilma Dykeman*
Explorations

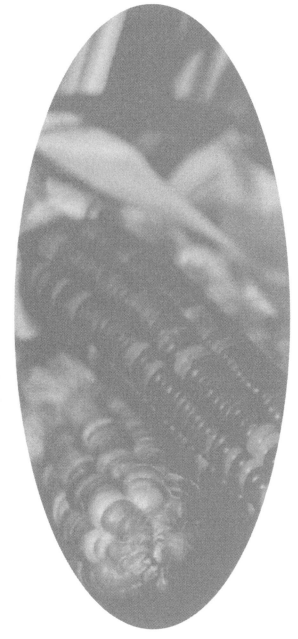

Beef in Burgundy

Ingredients

6	slices bacon, chopped
¼	cup olive oil
3	pounds beef sirloin, cut into 1½-inch cubes
4	cups dry burgundy
2	cups beef broth
2	tablespoons tomato paste
3	cloves of garlic, minced
½	teaspoon thyme
1	bay leaf
16	ounces fresh mushrooms, sliced
2	cups chopped onions
½	cup melted butter
½	cup flour
4	cups hot cooked white rice

Fry the bacon in a skillet until crisp. Remove the bacon with a slotted spoon, reserving bacon drippings. Discard bacon or reserve for another use. Add the olive oil to the pan drippings in the skillet. Brown the beef in the oil mixture, turning to brown all sides. Remove beef to a greased 4-quart casserole. Add 3 cups of the burgundy, beef broth, tomato paste, garlic, thyme and bay leaf. Heat the skillet with the remaining drippings over medium heat for 1 minute. Pour the remaining 1 cup burgundy into the hot skillet, scraping the bottom and side of the pan with a wooden spoon to release sediment. Remove the bay leaf. Add to the casserole.

Bake, covered, at 350 degrees for 2 hours, adding additional beef broth if needed for moisture. Stir in the mushrooms and onions. Bake at 350 degrees for 45 to 60 minutes longer or until beef is tender.

Blend the melted butter and flour in a skillet. Stir into the casserole. Bake at 350 degrees for 3 to 5 minutes longer. Serve over the rice.

yields eight servings

Three-Day Brisket

Ingredients

1	(4- to 7-pound) beef brisket
	Salt to taste
2	tablespoons liquid smoke
1½	cups chopped onion
2	cloves of garlic, minced
6	tablespoons butter
3	tablespoons brown sugar
1	(10-ounce) bottle catsup
½	cup water
2	tablespoons liquid smoke
¼	cup Worcestershire sauce
1	tablespoon each dry mustard and celery salt

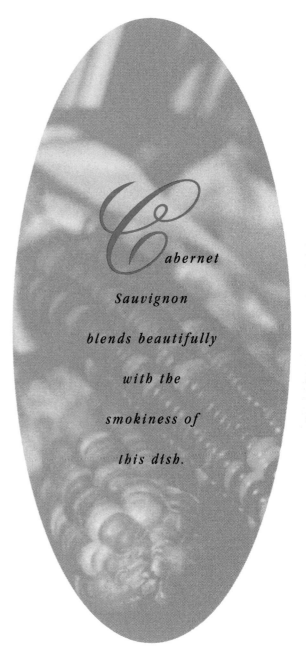

Cabernet Sauvignon blends beautifully with the smokiness of this dish.

Sprinkle the brisket on both sides with salt and 2 tablespoons liquid smoke. Seal in heavy-duty foil. Chill in refrigerator for 8 to 10 hours.

Open the foil. Add the onion and garlic to the brisket; seal the foil and place in a shallow baking pan.

Bake at 325 degrees for 5 hours. Cool briefly. Chill in refrigerator for 8 to 10 hours.

Remove the foil and discard the onion. Trim off fat; cut the brisket into slices. Place the slices on foil.

Melt the butter in a skillet. Stir in the brown sugar, catsup, water, remaining 2 tablespoons liquid smoke, Worcestershire sauce, mustard and celery salt until blended. Pour over the brisket; seal the foil.

Bake at 400 degrees for 10 minutes. Reduce the oven temperature to 325 degrees. Bake for 35 minutes longer.

yields twenty-four servings

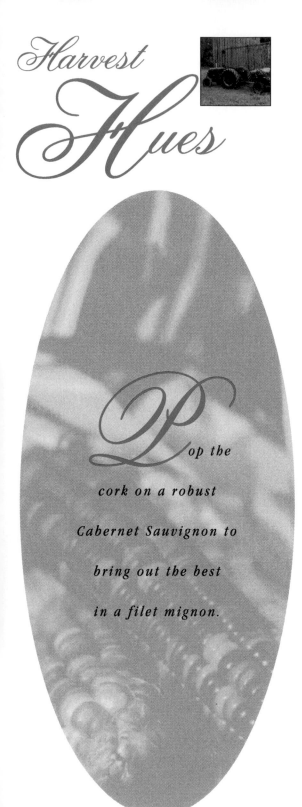

Pop the cork on a robust Cabernet Sauvignon to bring out the best in a filet mignon.

Bourbon Filets

Ingredients

2	cloves of garlic, minced
3	tablespoons butter
4	medium filets mignons
½	cup bourbon
8	ounces mushrooms, sliced
1	cup beef bouillon
1	cup cream or half-and-half
	Salt and pepper to taste

Sauté the garlic in the butter in a skillet until softened. Add the filets to the skillet. Cook until the filets are medium-rare to medium, turning to brown both sides. Pour in the bourbon. May ignite the bourbon and let the flame subside to add drama to the preparation. Remove filets to a hot platter, reserving the pan drippings. Place in a preheated 300-degree oven. Turn off the oven.

Cook the mushrooms in the pan drippings until tender. Add the bouillon. Bring to a boil. Add the cream gradually, whisking to mix well.

Simmer for 10 to 15 minutes or until thickened, stirring constantly. Add salt and pepper. Place the filets on a serving dish. Pour the sauce over filets. Serve immediately.

yields four servings

Veal Scaloppine

Ingredients

4	veal scallops
1	cup fine bread crumbs
2	tablespoons butter
2	tablespoons margarine
	Salt to taste
½	cup dry vermouth
2	tablespoons brandy
	Juice of 1 lemon

Dip the veal into bread crumbs to coat both sides. Fry the veal in hot butter and margarine in a skillet for 2 minutes on each side. Turn veal again, cooking for 3 minutes on each side or until golden brown. Remove to a hot serving plate, reserving the pan drippings. Add salt.

Add vermouth, brandy and lemon juice to the hot pan drippings. Boil rapidly for 1 minute, stirring constantly. Pour over the veal. Garnish with parsley and lemon slices.

yields two servings

An aged Italian Chianti is a splendid elegant wine to be served with veal, lamb or Cornish game hens.

Dark, centinel stargazer lilies placed in a crystal container with burgundy snapdragons, rust and gold Kangaroopaw and dark alstromeria accent an elegant dinner table.

Grilled Butterflied Leg of Lamb with Herbs

Ingredients

1	(8-pound) leg of lamb, boned, butterflied, trimmed of fat inside and out
	Salt and freshly ground pepper to taste
¼	cup olive oil
3	tablespoons mustard seeds
1	teaspoon cumin
1	tablespoon finely chopped garlic
4	sprigs of fresh thyme or 1 teaspoon dried thyme
1	teaspoon fennel seeds
2	tablespoons chopped fresh rosemary or 1 tablespoon dried rosemary
2	bay leaves, crumbled
¼	cup fresh lemon juice
2	tablespoons melted butter
¼	cup finely chopped parsley

Spread the lamb on a flat surface; sprinkle with salt and pepper. Pour the olive oil into a large baking dish. Add the lamb. Sprinkle on both sides with mustard seeds, cumin, garlic, thyme, fennel seeds, rosemary, bay leaves and lemon juice. Marinate, covered, for 1 to 6 hours in refrigerator. Bring to room temperature before cooking. Place lamb on a grill over hot coals, reserving the marinade. Cook for 10 to 15 minutes; turn and cook for 5 to 15 minutes longer or until done to taste. Cook for a total of 15 to 20 minutes for medium-rare lamb.

Bring reserved marinade to a boil in a saucepan. Stir in butter and parsley. Remove from the heat.

Let the lamb rest for 10 to 15 minutes before serving. Slice and serve with the pan gravy.

yields eight servings

Marinated London Broil

Ingredients

2	tablespoons brown sugar
3	tablespoons ground coriander
1	teaspoon salt
1	tablespoon chili powder
1	tablespoon minced garlic
1	teaspoon black pepper
1	teaspoon ground ginger
2	tablespoons lemon juice
2	tablespoons wine vinegar
1/4	cup soy sauce
1/4	cup sherry
1	tablespoon minced onion
1	(3-pound) London Broil

Combine the brown sugar, coriander, salt, chili powder, garlic, pepper, ginger, lemon juice, vinegar, soy sauce, sherry and onion in a bowl; mix well.

Place the London Broil in a shallow baking dish. Pour the marinade over the beef. Marinate, covered, in refrigerator for 8 to 10 hours.

Broil beef over hot coals for 4 to 5 minutes on each side. Cut diagonally across the grain into 1/4-inch slices.

yields six servings

Madeira Sauce

Ingredients

2	green onions, finely chopped
2	tablespoons butter
2½	tablespoons flour
1	(10-ounce) can beef broth
½	bay leaf
2	teaspoons tomato paste
	Pinch of herbes de Provence
	Pepper to taste
3	tablespoons madeira

Sauté the green onions in the butter in a skillet until clear. Stir in the flour. Cook for 2 minutes to form a roux, stirring constantly. Stir in the beef broth, bay leaf, tomato paste, herbes de Provence and pepper. Simmer for 5 minutes, stirring constantly; strain. Stir in the wine. Remove bay leaf. Serve with beef tenderloin.

yields one and one-fourth cups

Barbecue Sauce

Ingredients

1	(14-ounce) bottle catsup
½	(12-ounce) bottle chili sauce
¼	cup prepared mustard
½	tablespoon each dry mustard and soy sauce
¾	cup packed brown sugar
1	tablespoon each pepper and vegetable oil
¾	cup wine vinegar
½	cup lemon juice
¼	cup steak sauce
2	tablespoons Worcestershire sauce
	Dash of Tabasco sauce
½	can beer

Combine all ingredients in a large container; mix well. May store, covered, in refrigerator for several weeks.

yields six cups

Grilled Pork Tenderloin

Ingredients

½	cup peanut oil
⅓	cup soy sauce
¼	cup red wine vinegar
3	tablespoons lemon juice
2	tablespoons Worcestershire sauce
1	clove of garlic, minced
1	tablespoon chopped fresh parsley
1	tablespoon dry mustard
1½	teaspoons pepper
2	(¾- to 1-pound) pork tenderloins

A Sauvignon Blanc, Zinfandel or Pinot Noir would all complement this easy dish.

≫ Combine the oil, soy sauce, vinegar, lemon juice, Worcestershire sauce, garlic, parsley, dry mustard and pepper in a heavy-duty sealable plastic bag. Add tenderloins, turning to coat. Seal the plastic bag.

≫ Chill in refrigerator for 4 hours, turning occasionally; drain.

≫ Grill tenderloins 6 inches from medium-hot 300- to 400-degree coals for 12 to 14 minutes or until cooked through, turning once.

yields six servings

Harvest Hues

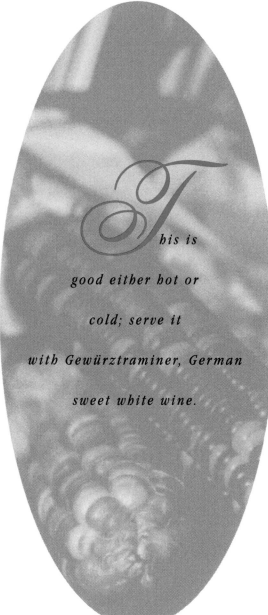

This is good either hot or cold; serve it with Gewürztraminer, German sweet white wine.

Chinese Pork Tenderloin

Ingredients

1	tablespoon sherry
2	tablespoons soy sauce
2	tablespoons brown sugar
1	teaspoon salt
½	teaspoon cinnamon
¼	teaspoon ginger
¼	teaspoon ground cloves
1	(2-pound) pork tenderloin

Combine the sherry, soy sauce, brown sugar, salt, cinnamon, ginger and cloves in a bowl; mix well. Place the pork tenderloin in a shallow dish. Pour the marinade over pork, turning to coat both sides.

Marinate, covered, in refrigerator for 2 hours, turning pork occasionally.

Remove the pork to a foil-lined baking pan, reserving the marinade.

Bake at 450 degrees for 10 minutes; baste pork with the marinade. Reduce the oven temperature to 325 degrees. Bake for 1 to 2 hours or until cooked through. Serve hot, cold or in a sandwich.

yields eight servings

Baked Stuffed Pork Tenderloin

Ingredients

¼	cup finely chopped celery
2	tablespoons finely chopped onion
2	tablespoons finely chopped green bell pepper
2	tablespoons butter
2	cups loosely packed soft bread crumbs
½	cup chopped apple
2	tablespoons raisins
¾	teaspoon salt
⅛	teaspoon pepper
1	teaspoon savory or poultry seasoning
1	tablespoon red currant jelly
2	(¾-pound) pork tenderloins
6	slices bacon

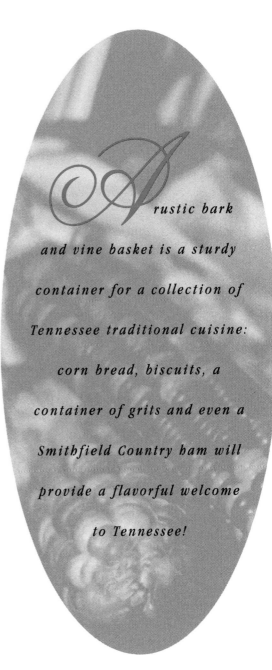

A rustic bark and vine basket is a sturdy container for a collection of Tennessee traditional cuisine: corn bread, biscuits, a container of grits and even a Smithfield Country ham will provide a flavorful welcome to Tennessee!

Sauté the celery, onion and green pepper in the butter in a large skillet until the onion is clear. Stir in the bread crumbs. Cook until the bread crumbs are coated, stirring gently. Remove from the heat. Add the apple, raisins, salt, pepper, savory and jelly; mix well.

Split each tenderloin almost through. Open up on a flat surface; pound with a meat mallet until thin and flattened.

Place the slices of bacon side by side on a flat surface. Arrange 1 tenderloin over bacon. Spread the stuffing over the top of tenderloin; cover with second tenderloin. Bring ends of bacon up over tenderloins to enclose; tie securely with a string. Place in a baking pan.

Bake at 325 degrees for 1¼ to 1½ hours or until cooked through.

yields six servings

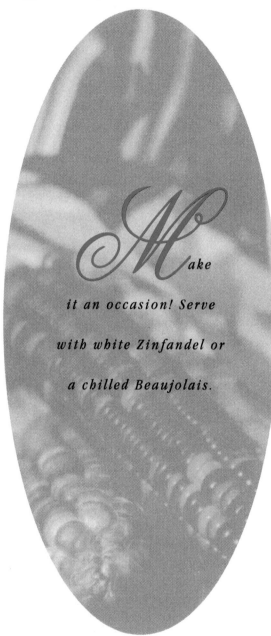

*M*ake

it an occasion! Serve

with white Zinfandel or

a chilled Beaujolais.

Stuffed Pizza

Ingredients

1	tablespoon sugar
1	envelope dry yeast
1¼	cups warm water
3½	cups flour
1½	teaspoons salt
¼	cup plus 1 tablespoon olive oil
1½	pounds broccoli, chopped
16	ounces mozzarella cheese, shredded
1	(28-ounce) can whole tomatoes, drained, mashed
1	teaspoon oregano
1½	teaspoons basil
1	clove of garlic, minced
¼	cup grated Romano cheese

Dissolve the sugar and yeast in warm water. Let stand at room temperature. Mix the flour and salt in a large bowl. Add ¼ cup olive oil and yeast; mix until the dough forms a ball. Knead for 3 to 4 minutes or until smooth and elastic. Place the dough in a floured bowl. Cover with plastic wrap and a towel. Let rise in a warm place for 1 hour or until doubled in bulk.

Punch dough down. Knead slightly on a floured surface. Divide dough into 2 portions, 1 slightly larger. Roll larger portion 2 to 3 inches larger than a 12-inch pizza pan. Place dough on pan so that it overlaps by 1 inch. Trim excess dough and discard. Roll the remaining portion of dough to the same size as pizza pan.

Blanch the broccoli in boiling water for 2 minutes; drain. Place on pizza crust; sprinkle mozzarella cheese over the top. Arrange remaining dough over top, crimping edges to form a thick edge and cutting 3 or 4 vents. Combine the tomatoes, 1 tablespoon olive oil, oregano, basil, garlic and Romano cheese in a bowl; mix well. Spoon over the top of the stuffed pizza.

Bake at 450 degrees on the lowest oven rack for 10 minutes. Move to the middle rack. Bake for 25 minutes longer or until brown.

yields eight servings

Boursin-Stuffed Chicken Breasts

Ingredients

4	whole boneless skinless chicken breasts
½	cup melted butter
¼	cup white wine
1	cup Italian bread crumbs
	Salt and pepper to taste
8	tablespoons boursin cheese
8	sprigs of fresh parsley
	Dash of paprika

Rinse the chicken; pat dry. Cut each chicken breast into halves. Pound each piece of chicken with a meat mallet until of even thickness. Combine the melted butter and wine in a shallow bowl. Place the bread crumbs in a shallow bowl. Dip each piece of chicken into the wine mixture; coat with the bread crumbs. Sprinkle with salt and pepper.

Place 1 tablespoon boursin cheese in the center of each piece of chicken. Roll chicken to enclose cheese; secure with a wooden pick and place seam side down in a buttered baking dish. Drizzle with the remaining wine mixture.

Bake at 450 degrees for 20 minutes or until chicken is tender and golden brown. Top with the parsley and sprinkle with paprika. Serve immediately.

yields eight servings

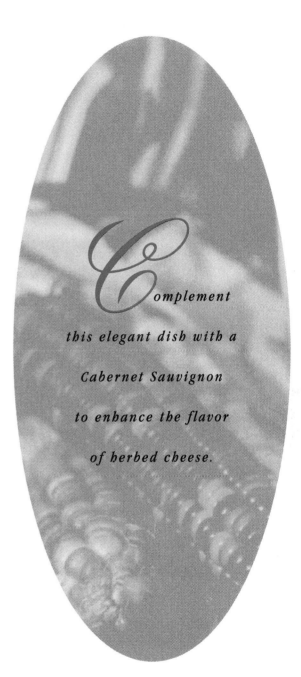

Complement this elegant dish with a Cabernet Sauvignon to enhance the flavor of herbed cheese.

Harvest Hues

*P*lace

a California Zinfandel

in the refrigerator

to chill while

the chicken marinates.

Peppered Chicken Breasts with Rosemary and Garlic

Ingredients

2	tablespoons fresh lemon juice
2	tablespoons olive oil
½	teaspoon rosemary
⅛	(to ¼) teaspoon crushed hot red pepper
½	(to 1) teaspoon coarsely cracked black pepper
4	cloves of garlic, minced
4	boneless skinless chicken breasts halves

Combine the lemon juice, olive oil, rosemary, red pepper, black pepper and garlic in a bowl just large enough to hold chicken; mix well. Rinse the chicken; pat dry. Add the chicken to the marinade, turning to coat.

Marinate, covered, in refrigerator for 1 hour, turning 1 or 2 times; drain.

Grill chicken over medium-hot coals until cooked through.

yields four servings

Sherried Chicken Breasts

Ingredients

6	large skinless chicken breasts
¾	teaspoon salt
	Pepper to taste
	Paprika to taste
1	cup chicken bouillon
½	cup melted margarine
⅓	cup sherry
⅓	pound fresh mushrooms, sliced

Rinse the chicken; pat dry. Sprinkle with the salt, pepper and paprika. Arrange in a baking pan. Pour bouillon and margarine over the chicken.

Bake at 325 degrees for 1 hour, basting with pan drippings 3 or 4 times. Pour the sherry over chicken.

Bake for 30 minutes longer.

Sauté the mushrooms in a skillet until brown. Arrange chicken on serving platter; top with the mushrooms.

yields six servings

A California Chardonnay or white Burgundy goes well with this.

J ust add a Johannisberg Riesling or a Chenin Blanc for a festive one-dish meal.

Vermouth-Poached Chicken with Rice

Ingredients

1	cup uncooked rice
2	cups chicken broth
2	teaspoons salt
4	whole boneless skinless chicken breasts
½	teaspoon pepper
3	medium carrots, sliced
2	stalks celery, thinly sliced
1	medium onion, thinly sliced
4	cloves of garlic, minced
2	tablespoons chopped fresh parsley
⅔	cup dry vermouth
½	cup sour cream

Combine the rice, chicken broth and 1 teaspoon of the salt in a buttered casserole. Cover the casserole.

Rinse the chicken; pat dry. Cut into halves; arrange in a greased 2-quart casserole. Sprinkle with the remaining 1 teaspoon salt and pepper. Arrange carrots, celery, onion, garlic and parsley over chicken; pour in vermouth. Cover the casserole. Place both casseroles in the oven.

Bake at 375 degrees for 30 minutes or until chicken is tender. Remove chicken; arrange over the rice.

Stir the sour cream into the vegetables.

Bake for 2 to 3 minutes longer or until heated through. Spoon the vegetable mixture over chicken and rice.

yields six servings

Chicken Marsala

Ingredients

4	boneless skinless chicken breast halves
¼	cup egg substitute
1	cup nonfat saltine cracker crumbs
1	teaspoon minced garlic
¼	cup liquid Butter Buds
¼	cup marsala or red cooking wine
1	chicken bouillon cube
	Dash of ground pepper
2	tablespoons chopped parsley

A nice low-fat variation of this classic recipe.

Rinse the chicken; pat dry. Pound each piece of chicken with meat mallet to ¼-inch thickness. Place the egg substitute in a shallow bowl. Place the cracker crumbs in a shallow bowl. Dip the chicken in egg substitute; coat with the cracker crumbs.

Sauté the garlic in 2 tablespoons liquid Butter Buds in a skillet sprayed with nonstick cooking spray for 1 to 2 minutes. Add the chicken. Cook for 6 minutes or until chicken is tender, turning once. Remove to a warm platter. Keep warm in a 250-degree oven.

Add wine to pan drippings, stirring to loosen sediment in skillet. Add bouillon cube, stirring until dissolved. Add pepper and parsley. Add remaining Butter Buds if too dry. Cook until mixture boils and thickens, stirring constantly. Spoon over chicken. Serve immediately.

yields four servings

A simple salad with a little body and kick is made by combining one 6-ounce package sugar-free raspberry gelatin, 2 cups boiling water and 2 cups no-sugar-added applesauce. A nice accompaniment with the Chicken Pot Pie.

Chicken Pot Pie

Ingredients

4	chicken breasts
1	stalk celery, coarsely chopped
1	large carrot, coarsely chopped
1	bay leaf
6	tablespoons butter
6	tablespoons flour
1	(10-ounce) package frozen peas
2	carrots, finely chopped
	Dash of poultry seasoning or thyme
	Dash of salt and white pepper
1	unbaked all ready pie pastry

Rinse the chicken. Combine the chicken, celery, coarsely chopped carrot, bay leaf and enough water to cover in a saucepan. Simmer, covered, for 40 minutes or until chicken is tender; drain, reserving 3 cups chicken broth. Chop chicken.

Melt the butter in a saucepan. Stir in the flour until well mixed. Cook for 1 minute, stirring constantly. Add the reserved chicken broth; mix well. Simmer until thickened, stirring frequently.

Cook the frozen peas with the finely chopped carrots using package directions for 10 minutes or until tender-crisp; drain. Add poultry seasoning, salt and pepper. Combine with the chicken and the broth mixture in the saucepan. Remove the bay leaf. Spoon into a buttered baking dish; top with the pie pastry, trimming to fit and cutting vents.

Bake at 350 degrees for 35 to 45 minutes or until bubbly and golden brown. May add 1 small potato, chopped, to peas and carrots and ½ cup sautéed onion and ½ cup sautéed celery to the pot pie.

yields four servings

Chicken Enchiladas

Ingredients

8	(6-inch) tortillas
½	cup chopped onion
4	cloves of garlic, minced
1	teaspoon coriander
¼	teaspoon pepper
2	tablespoons margarine or butter
3	tablespoons flour
1	cup sour cream
2	cups chicken broth
1	(or 2) (10-ounce) cans jalapeños
1	cup shredded Monterey Jack cheese
2	cups chopped cooked chicken
1	cup shredded Cheddar cheese

Wrap the tortillas in foil.

Bake at 350 degrees for 10 to 15 minutes or until softened.

Sauté the onion and garlic with coriander and pepper in margarine in a large skillet until onion is tender. Stir the flour into sour cream in a bowl. Add to the sautéed vegetables; mix well. Stir in the broth and jalapeños. Cook until thickened, stirring constantly. Remove from the heat. Stir in ½ cup of the Monterey Jack Cheese.

Combine ½ cup of the sauce and chicken in bowl; mix well. Place about ¼ cup chicken mixture on each tortilla; roll tortilla to enclose filling. Place seam side down in a greased 7x11-inch baking dish; cover with remaining sauce.

Bake, covered, at 350 degrees for 30 to 35 minutes or until heated through. Sprinkle with remaining Monterey Jack cheese and Cheddar cheese. Bake, uncovered, at 350 degrees for 5 minutes longer or until cheese is melted. Garnish with sliced olives, chopped tomatoes and sliced green onions. Let stand for 10 minutes before serving. May substitute one 4-ounce can green chiles for jalapeños.

yields four servings

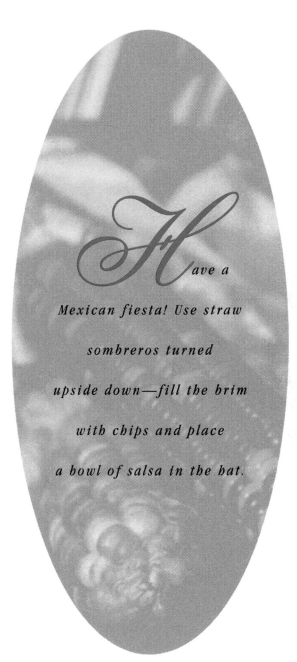

Have a Mexican fiesta! Use straw sombreros turned upside down—fill the brim with chips and place a bowl of salsa in the hat.

A casual twist on an elegant entrée ... finger lickin' good!

Texas-Style Cornish Game Hens

Ingredients

4	(1¼-pound) Cornish game hens
½	teaspoon salt
1	(or 2) cloves of garlic, minced
1	teaspoon chili powder
½	cup apple jelly
½	cup catsup
1	tablespoon vinegar

Rinse Cornish game hens; pat dry. Cut into halves. Combine salt, garlic and chili powder in bowl. Sprinkle both sides of Cornish game hens.

Grill over medium-hot coals for 45 minutes, turning occasionally.

Combine the apple jelly, catsup and vinegar in a saucepan. Cook over medium heat until the jelly melts, stirring constantly. Brush Cornish game hens with the sauce.

Grill for 15 minutes longer, turning and basting with sauce frequently.

yields six servings

Elegant Orange Roughy

Ingredients

4	orange roughy fillets
2	tablespoons butter
1	tablespoon lemon juice
6	green onions, chopped
1	tablespoon butter
25	large cooked peeled shrimp
1	teaspoon lemon juice
15	ounces crab meat, shredded
¼	cup chopped parsley

Cook the fish fillets in 2 tablespoons butter in a skillet until fish flakes easily. Remove to a warm platter; drizzle with 1 tablespoon lemon juice. Keep warm in a 250-degree oven.

Sauté the green onions in 1 tablespoon butter in a sauté pan. Add shrimp and 1 teaspoon lemon juice. Cook for 10 minutes, stirring frequently. Add crab meat and 2 tablespoons of the parsley. Cook until of serving temperature. Spoon crab mixture over orange roughy; sprinkle with remaining parsley. Serve warm.

yields four servings

Our Strawberry-Spinach Salad is a colorful accompaniment.

Harvest Hues

California

Pinot Noir or

French red Burgundy

adds just

the right touch.

Marinated Grilled Tuna

Ingredients

½	cup soy sauce
½	cup dry sherry
1	tablespoon lemon juice
¼	cup vegetable oil
1	clove of garlic, minced
8	(½-inch-thick) tuna fillets

Combine the soy sauce, sherry, lemon juice, oil and garlic in a shallow bowl. Add tuna fillets, turning to coat both sides.

Marinate, covered, in refrigerator for 1 to 2 hours; drain. Do not marinate for longer than 2 hours or the flavor of the marinade will be too strong.

Grill or broil for 5 to 6 minutes on each side or until tuna flakes easily.

yields eight servings

Maryland Crab Cakes with Herb Mayonnaise

Ingredients

1	pound lump crab meat, shell removed
1	cup Italian bread crumbs
1	large egg, beaten
¼	cup mayonnaise
½	teaspoon salt
¼	teaspoon white pepper
1	teaspoon Worcestershire sauce
1	teaspoon dry mustard
¼	cup chopped fresh parsley
2	egg yolks, at room temperature
2	tablespoons red wine vinegar
1	tablespoon Dijon mustard
1	tablespoon chopped fresh parsley
1	tablespoon chopped fresh tarragon
¼	teaspoon salt
¾	cup extra-virgin olive oil

A chilled California Sauvignon Blanc is the perfect complement for these traditional crab cakes.

≈ Combine the crab meat, bread crumbs, egg, mayonnaise, salt, pepper, Worcestershire sauce, dry mustard and ¼ cup parsley in a bowl; mix well. Shape into 8 patties; place in a shallow pan. Chill, covered, in refrigerator for 30 minutes.

≈ Combine the egg yolks, vinegar, Dijon mustard, 1 tablespoon parsley, tarragon, salt and olive oil in a food processor or blender container; process until blended. Chill, covered, in refrigerator until serving time.

≈ Place the crab cakes on a rack in a broiler pan. Broil for 5 minutes on each side, turning once. Serve immediately with herb mayonnaise. Garnish with lemon wedges.

yields eight servings

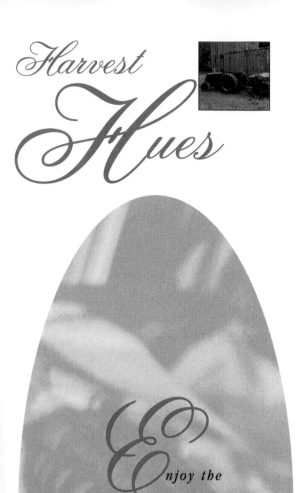

Enjoy the

luxury of lobster with

a California Pinot

Noir or red Burgundy.

Lobster Linguini in Tomato Cream Sauce

Ingredients

½	cup minced shallots
⅛	teaspoon red pepper flakes
2	tablespoons butter
¼	teaspoon salt
3	(14-ounce) cans plum tomatoes
1	cup whipping cream
4	lobster tails, cooked, chopped
16	ounces linguini
2	tablespoons chopped parsley

Sauté the shallots with red pepper in the butter in a large skillet for 5 minutes or until tender. Add the salt and undrained tomatoes. Cook over high heat for 8 to 10 minutes or until almost all the liquid is evaporated, crushing the tomatoes with a spoon. Stir in the cream. Bring to a boil and boil for 1 minute, stirring constantly. Reduce the heat to low. Stir in the lobster. Cook for 4 to 5 minutes or until heated through. Adjust the seasonings.

Cook the linguini using package directions; drain. Add the lobster sauce and parsley; toss lightly to mix. Serve immediately.

yields four servings

Cajun Seafood Carbonara

Ingredients

8	ounces bacon, partially frozen
2	tablespoons coarsely chopped garlic
1	each medium red and green bell pepper, chopped
½	pound andouille sausage, chopped
1	small red onion, chopped
3	tablespoons Cajun spice blend
½	cup Durkee red hot sauce
1	pound each fresh peeled shrimp and fresh scallops
2	teaspoons paprika
½	cup butter
¼	cup flour
½	cup white wine
4	cups whipping cream
3	cups freshly grated Parmesan cheese
8	ounces lump crab meat, shell removed
2	pounds linguini, cooked

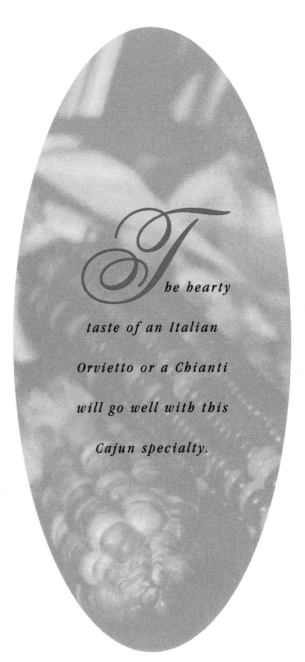

The hearty taste of an Italian Orvietto or a Chianti will go well with this Cajun specialty.

Coarsely chop the bacon. Fry bacon in a large skillet just until starting to brown. Add the garlic. Fry until clear. Add the red pepper, green pepper, sausage, red onion, 2 tablespoons of the Cajun spice blend and ¼ cup of the Durkee red hot sauce. Reduce the heat to low. Cook for 10 minutes, stirring frequently; drain. Remove bacon mixture to a bowl.

Sauté the shrimp and scallops with paprika and the remaining 1 tablespoon Cajun spice blend in the butter in a skillet for 1 minute or until the seafood is partially cooked. Mix flour and wine together. Add to the seafood, stirring until well mixed. Cook for 2 minutes over low heat, stirring constantly. Add bacon mixture and cream. Cook over medium heat for 3 to 5 minutes, stirring constantly. Stir in the Parmesan cheese and crab meat just until blended. Adjust the seasonings, adding the remaining Durkee red hot sauce if desired. Serve the seafood sauce over the hot cooked linguini on a serving platter.

yields ten servings

Harvest Hues

*A*dd a

salad and a

Beaujolais Villages

for a perfect meal.

Sea Scallops Florentine

Ingredients

2	(12-ounce) bunches fresh spinach
2	tablespoons fresh orange juice
1	teaspoon Dijon mustard
	Freshly ground black pepper to taste
2	tablespoons extra-virgin olive oil
2	tablespoons chopped fresh chives
	Salt to taste
1½	pounds sea scallops
2	tablespoons pure olive oil
2	teaspoons finely grated orange peel

Remove the tough stems from the spinach; rinse the spinach well and shake off excess water. Place in a saucepan.

Combine orange juice, mustard, and pepper in a bowl; whisk well to mix. Add 2 tablespoons of the olive oil in a slow steady stream while whisking. Stir in 1 tablespoon of the chives and salt.

Rinse scallops; pat dry. Cook scallops ½ at a time in 2 tablespoons olive oil in a large nonstick skillet until opaque and golden brown on edges, turning 1 time. Remove to a warm platter. Keep warm in a 200-degree oven.

Cook spinach, covered, in the saucepan over medium heat for 3 minutes, stirring 1 time; drain. Place on a serving platter. Spoon the scallops onto the spinach; top with the orange juice sauce. Sprinkle with the remaining chives and orange peel.

yields six servings

Shrimp Thermidor

Ingredients

¼	cup plus 1 tablespoon butter
⅓	cup plus 3 tablespoons flour
1	teaspoon salt
1	teaspoon minced onion
1	teaspoon dry mustard
¼	cup minced parsley
2	cups whipping cream
½	cup sherry
¼	cup shredded Swiss cheese
	Pepper to taste
1	pound peeled, boiled medium shrimp

Melt the butter in a large skillet. Blend in the flour, salt, onion, mustard and parsley. Stir in the cream. Cook over low heat until thickened, stirring constantly. Stir in the sherry, Swiss cheese and pepper. Add the shrimp; heat to serving temperature, stirring frequently. Serve over rice.

yields four servings

The crisp taste of a Pinot Blanc or Chardonnay will be a good foil for this rich entrée.

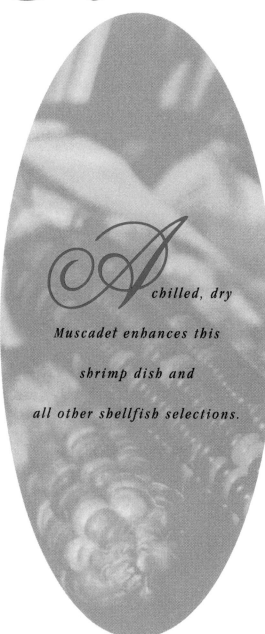

A chilled, dry Muscadet enhances this shrimp dish and all other shellfish selections.

Ocean Spring Shrimp

Ingredients

1	pound shrimp, cooked, peeled, deveined
	Salt and pepper to taste
8	ounces mushrooms, sliced
3	tablespoons butter
1	tablespoon flour
1	cup sour cream
5	tablespoons butter, softened
1	teaspoon soy sauce
¼	cup grated Parmesan cheese
1	teaspoon paprika

Place the shrimp in 1 layer in a buttered shallow baking dish just large enough to hold them. Sprinkle with salt and pepper.

Sauté the mushrooms in 3 tablespoons butter in a skillet; remove to a bowl. Sprinkle with flour, tossing to coat. Add the sour cream, butter and soy sauce. Pour the mushroom mixture over the shrimp; sprinkle with Parmesan cheese and paprika.

Bake at 400 degrees for 10 minutes.

yields four servings

Mustard Mint Sauce

Ingredients

1	tablespoon Dijon mustard
1	tablespoon (or less) coarse-grain mustard
3	tablespoons white wine vinegar
¼	cup packed fresh mint leaves
¾	cup olive oil

Combine the Dijon and coarse-grain mustards, vinegar and mint leaves in a blender container. Add the oil in a fine steady stream, processing until smooth.

yields one cup

Lemon-Chive Topping

Ingredients

¾	cup mayonnaise
2	tablespoons lemon juice
1	tablespoon chopped chives
1	egg white, stiffly beaten

Combine the mayonnaise, lemon juice and chives in a bowl; mix well. Fold in stiffly beaten egg white gently. Spoon the mixture over cooked fish. Broil until top is puffed and golden brown. Serve immediately.

yields one cup

This Mustard Mint Sauce is delicious with salmon or swordfish.

Soups

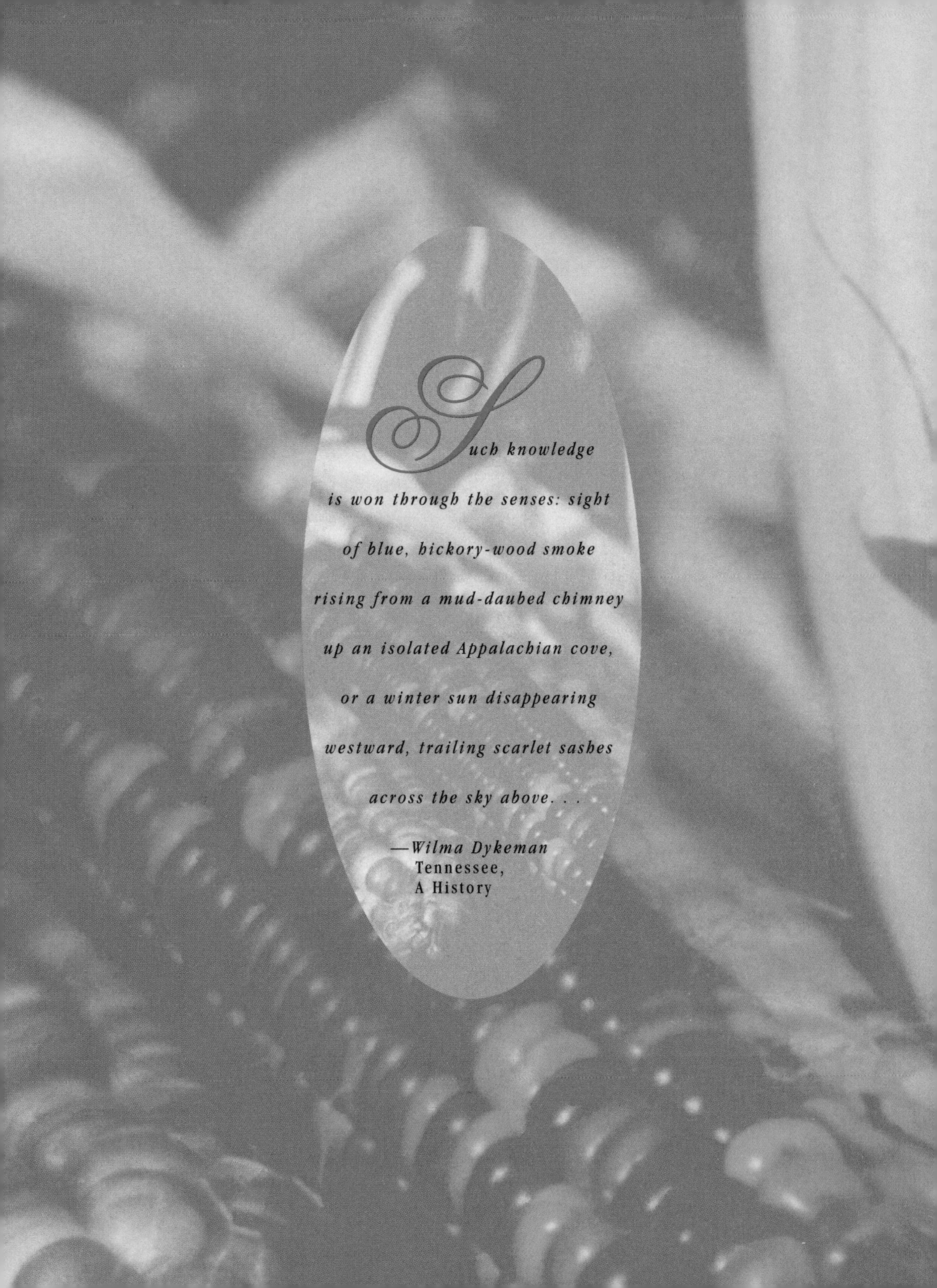

Such knowledge

is won through the senses: sight

of blue, hickory-wood smoke

rising from a mud-daubed chimney

up an isolated Appalachian cove,

or a winter sun disappearing

westward, trailing scarlet sashes

across the sky above. . .

—*Wilma Dykeman*
Tennessee,
A History

Harvest Hues

A tasty way to cool off on a hot summer night.

Chilled Zucchini Soup

Ingredients

3	medium zucchini, sliced
3	stalks celery, sliced
2	green onions with tops, sliced
1	carrot, peeled, sliced
1	clove of garlic, minced
1	teaspoon chopped parsley
½	teaspoon dillweed
¼	teaspoon thyme
1	teaspoon salt
¼	teaspoon pepper
6	cups chicken broth
1½	cups sour cream
	Dillweed

Combine the zucchini, celery, green onions, carrot, garlic, parsley, ½ teaspoon dillweed, thyme, salt, pepper and chicken broth in a saucepan. Simmer for 10 minutes or until the vegetables are tender-crisp. Reserve several slices of the vegetables in a bowl.

Purée the remaining vegetables and broth in a blender. Add 1 cup of the sour cream; process until smooth. Spoon into a bowl with the reserved vegetable slices. Chill, covered, until thoroughly chilled. Spoon into serving bowls. Serve with a dollop of sour cream sprinkled with dillweed.

yields six servings

Lentil Soup

Ingredients

1	(16-ounce) package dried lentils
1	pound Italian sausage
2	large onions, chopped
6	medium carrots, chopped
1½	cups chopped celery
1	tablespoon salt
4	quarts water
1	teaspoon pepper
1	teaspoon thyme
2	bay leaves
4	large potatoes, coarsely grated

Rinse and sort the lentils. Combine the lentils and enough water to cover by 1 to 2 inches in a 4-quart saucepan. Let soak for 4 to 8 hours; drain and rinse.

Brown the sausage in a skillet, pressing with a potato masher to break into small pieces.

Combine the onions, carrots and celery in a food processor container; process until finely chopped. Add to the sausage. Cook until the vegetables are tender-crisp.

Combine the sausage mixture, lentils, salt, water, pepper, thyme and bay leaves in a large stockpot. Simmer for 1 to 1½ hours, stirring occasionally. Add the potatoes. Simmer for 30 minutes, stirring occasionally. Remove the bay leaves before serving.

yields twenty servings

*F*resh baked

bread and a Caesar

salad make this a warm and

fuzzy winter meal.

Potato Soup

Ingredients

5	medium potatoes, peeled, finely chopped
1	small onion, chopped
1	stalk celery, chopped
2	teaspoons celery salt
1	teaspoon seasoned salt
1	teaspoon dried basil
¼	teaspoon pepper
2	tablespoons dried parsley flakes
2	chicken-flavor bouillon cubes
4	cups water
4	slices bacon
2	tablespoons flour
1½	cups milk

Combine the potatoes, onion, celery, celery salt, seasoned salt, basil, pepper, parsley flakes, bouillon cubes and water in a stockpot. Bring to a boil. Reduce the heat. Simmer, covered, for 20 minutes, stirring occasionally.

Fry the bacon in a skillet until crisp; drain, reserving 3 tablespoons bacon drippings in skillet. Crumble the bacon. Add the flour to bacon drippings, stirring until well mixed. Cook for 1 minute, stirring constantly. Add the milk gradually. Cook over medium heat until thickened, stirring constantly. Stir the milk mixture and crumbled bacon into the soup. Simmer, uncovered, for 15 minutes, stirring frequently.

yields eight servings

Jack-O'-Lantern Soup

Ingredients

¼	cup butter
3	cups chicken broth
2	cups canned pumpkin
2	cups puréed sweet potatoes
½	cup smooth peanut butter
¼	cup Jack Daniel's whiskey
1½	teaspoons allspice
5	tablespoons sorghum molasses
1	teaspoon cinnamon

Melt the butter in a stockpot. Add chicken broth; mix well. Stir in the pumpkin, sweet potatoes, peanut butter, whiskey, allspice, molasses and cinnamon. Cook until of serving temperature. Spoon into bowls. Garnish with a dollop of sour cream and chopped fresh chives.

yields nine servings

Vegetable Soup

Ingredients

1	pound lean stew beef and soup bone
1½	(to 2) quarts water
1	(16-ounce) can tomatoes
1	(6-ounce) can tomato sauce
1	teaspoon salt
1	teaspoon pepper
1	tablespoon marjoram
1	tablespoon basil
2	bay leaves
½	teaspoon parsley
1	(10-ounce) package mixed vegetables
1	onion, chopped
1	potato, coarsely chopped

Combine the stew beef, soup bone and water in a stockpot. Simmer for 30 minutes, stirring occasionally. Add the tomatoes, tomato sauce, salt, pepper, marjoram, basil, bay leaves and parsley. Cook for 15 minutes, stirring occasionally.

Add the mixed vegetables, onion and potato. Cook, covered, for 2 to 2½ hours, stirring occasionally. Remove the bay leaves. Spoon into bowls. Garnish with Parmesan cheese. May substitute dry onion soup mix for the onion. Add corn, carrot, celery, okra or any vegetable of your choice when adding mixed vegetables.

yields twelve servings

Chili

Ingredients

8	ounces bacon
1	pound ground chuck beef
1	pound cubed round steak
1	pound cubed pork steak
1	stalk celery, chopped
2	onions, chopped
1	green bell pepper, chopped
1	(30-ounce) can tomatoes
3	tablespoons catsup
1	teaspoon Worcestershire sauce
1	(16-ounce) can kidney beans, rinsed, drained
1	tablespoon prepared mustard
¼	cup sugar
1	jalapeño, finely chopped
1	teaspoon chili powder

A flavorful blend of tastes for that meat lover in your life.

Fry the bacon in a skillet; drain and crumble. Brown the ground beef in a skillet, stirring until crumbly; drain. Brown the round steak and pork in a skillet; drain. Sauté the celery, onions and green pepper in a skillet until soft.

Combine the crumbled bacon, ground beef, round steak, pork, celery, onions, green pepper, undrained tomatoes, catsup, Worcestershire sauce, kidney beans, mustard, sugar, jalapeño and chili powder in a stockpot; mix well. Bring to a boil; reduce the heat. Simmer for 3 hours, stirring occasionally. Spoon into serving bowls.

yields ten servings

White Chicken Chili

Ingredients

1	pound dried white navy beans
4	boneless skinless chicken breasts
1	(10-ounce) can chicken broth
1	teaspoon salt
1½	medium onions, chopped
2	cloves of garlic, minced
1	tablespoon vegetable oil
1	(4-ounce) can chopped green chiles
2	teaspoons each cumin, dried oregano and coriander
	Pinch each of ground cloves and cayenne
½	cup shredded Monterey Jack cheese
4	green onions, thinly sliced

Rinse and sort the beans. Combine the beans with enough water to cover by 1 to 2 inches in a large stockpot. Let soak for 8 to 10 hours; drain.

Combine the chicken with enough water to cover in a saucepan. Bring to a boil; reduce the heat. Simmer, covered, for 10 to 15 minutes or until chicken is tender; drain, reserving broth. Cool the chicken slightly; cut into bite-size pieces. Chill in refrigerator.

Add enough canned chicken broth to reserved broth to measure 6 cups. Combine the 6 cups broth, beans, salt and half the onions and garlic in a large stockpot. Simmer, covered, for 1½ to 2 hours or until the beans are tender, stirring occasionally and adding additional broth if needed.

Sauté the remaining onions and garlic in hot oil in a skillet until tender. Add the green chiles, cumin, oregano, coriander, cloves and cayenne; mix well. Cook for 20 minutes over low heat, stirring frequently. Add to the bean mixture. Stir in the chopped chicken. Bring to serving temperature. Spoon into bowls. Top with cheese and green onions.

yields six servings

Pink Chili

Ingredients

2	cups dried navy beans
6	cups water
8	chicken bouillon cubes
2	onions, coarsely chopped
1	(4-ounce) can chopped green chiles
1	(10-ounce) can tomatoes with green chiles
2	teaspoons cumin
1½	teaspoons oregano
1	tablespoon chili powder
4	cups shredded cooked chicken breast

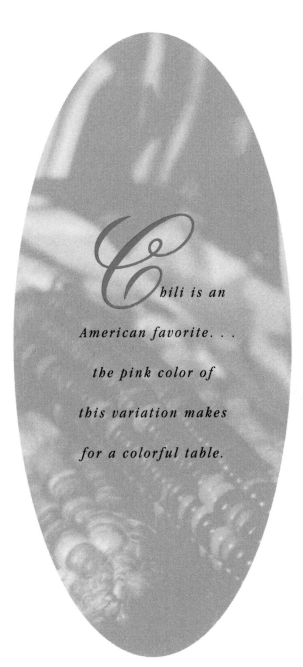

Chili is an American favorite. . . the pink color of this variation makes for a colorful table.

Rinse and sort the beans. Combine the beans and enough water to cover by 1 to 2 inches in a large stockpot. Let soak for 8 to 10 hours; drain.

Combine the beans, 6 cups water, bouillon cubes, onions, green chiles, tomatoes, cumin, oregano and chili powder in a stockpot. Simmer over medium heat for 1 hour or until the beans are tender, stirring occasionally. Add the chicken. Simmer, covered, over low heat for 1 hour, stirring occasionally. Spoon into bowls. May substitute canned beans for dried.

yields six servings

Corn Chowder

Ingredients

4	slices bacon, chopped
1	cup water
1	onion, chopped
4	(to 6) potatoes, chopped
1	(16-ounce) package frozen corn, thawed
1	cup whipping cream
1	teaspoon sugar
¼	cup butter
2	cups milk
2½	teaspoons salt
½	teaspoon pepper

Sauté the chopped bacon in a large skillet until brown. Add the water, onion and potatoes. Simmer over low heat for 20 minutes, stirring frequently.

Combine the corn, cream, sugar and butter in a stockpot. Simmer, covered, for 20 minutes, stirring occasionally. Add the potato mixture; mix well. Add the milk, salt and pepper. Heat to serving temperature. Do not boil.

yields ten servings

Salmon Chowder

Ingredients

½	cup chopped onion
½	cup chopped celery
½	cup chopped green bell pepper
3	tablespoons butter
1	cup finely chopped potatoes
1	cup finely chopped carrots
2	cups chicken broth
1½	teaspoons salt
1	clove of garlic, minced
¾	teaspoon pepper
½	teaspoon dillseeds
½	medium zucchini, finely chopped
1	(8-ounce) salmon fillet, cooked, flaked
1	(15-ounce) can cream-style corn
1	(12-ounce) can evaporated milk

Serve a Sauvignon Blanc or Pinot Grigio with this chowder to tantalize your taste buds.

Sauté the onion, celery and green pepper in the butter in a large skillet until tender. Stir in the potatoes, carrots, chicken broth, salt, garlic, pepper and dillseeds. Simmer, covered, for 20 to 30 minutes or until the potatoes are tender, stirring frequently. Stir in the zucchini. Remove from the heat; let stand to cool for 5 minutes. Add the salmon, corn and evaporated milk. Heat to serving temperature. Spoon into bowls.

May freeze after adding the zucchini and cooling.

yields six servings

Harvest Hues

Hollowed-out gourd filled with big, Rover mums, yellow golden asters and small branches of leaves makes for a wonderful fall display.

Sherried Crab Bisque

Ingredients

1	medium carrot, shredded
¼	cup grated onion
2	tablespoons unsalted butter
2	tablespoons flour
2	cups chicken broth
2	cups half-and-half
1	tablespoon dry sherry
2	dashes of Tabasco sauce
1	pound lump crab meat, shell removed
1	tablespoon chopped fresh parsley
	Salt to taste

Sauté the carrot and onion in the butter in a stockpot over low heat just until softened. Sprinkle in the flour, stirring to mix well. Cook for 5 minutes, stirring constantly; do not brown. Stir in the chicken broth, half-and-half, sherry and Tabasco sauce. Simmer for 10 minutes, stirring occasionally. Stir in the crab meat. Heat to serving temperature. Add parsley and salt. Adjust the seasonings. Spoon into bowls. Serve with a pitcher of sherry to add to the soup as desired.

yields six servings

Shrimp Bisque

Ingredients

¼	cup chopped green bell pepper
1	small onion, chopped
¼	cup plus 2 tablespoons butter
¼	cup chopped green onions with tops
2	tablespoons chopped parsley
1½	cups sliced fresh mushrooms
2	tablespoons flour
1	cup milk
1	teaspoon salt
⅛	teaspoon white pepper
	Dash of Tabasco sauce
1½	cups half-and-half
1½	cups peeled cooked small shrimp
¼	cup dry sherry

Sauté the green pepper and onion in the ¼ cup butter in a skillet until tender. Add the green onions, parsley and mushrooms. Sauté for 5 minutes or until soft. Add the 2 tablespoons butter. Cook until melted. Stir in the flour until well mixed. Add the milk.

Cook until thickened, stirring constantly. Stir in the salt, pepper, Tabasco sauce and half-and-half. Bring to a boil. Reduce the heat. Add the shrimp and sherry. Simmer, uncovered, for 5 minutes, stirring frequently.

yields four servings

Harvest Hues

*W*elcome a new neighbor or remember a friend with this soup mix. Store in plastic bags and wrap up with a pretty ribbon.

Chicken Noodle Soup Mix

Ingredients

1	cup uncooked fine egg noodles
1	tablespoon dried minced onion
2½	tablespoons chicken bouillon granules
1	teaspoon pepper
¼	teaspoon dried whole thyme
⅛	teaspoon celery seeds
⅛	teaspoon garlic powder
1	bay leaf

∽ Combine the egg noodles, minced onion, chicken bouillon, pepper, thyme, celery seeds, garlic powder and bay leaf in a bowl. Store in a sealable plastic bag.

∽ To prepare the soup, combine the mix, 8 cups water and 1 finely chopped carrot in a saucepan. Bring to a boil. Reduce the heat; simmer for 15 minutes, stirring occasionally. Discard the bay leaf. Stir in 3 cups chopped cooked chicken. Simmer for 5 minutes longer, stirring occasionally.

yields eight servings

Brunswick Stew

Ingredients

1	(3-pound) chicken, cut up
2	ounces salt pork
3	(16-ounce) cans tomatoes, drained
2	(16-ounce) cans cream-style corn
2	(16-ounce) cans lima beans, drained
2	teaspoons salt
	Pepper to taste
1	tablespoon tarragon
1	teaspoon basil
1	tablespoon Worcestershire sauce
1	tablespoon sugar
2	tablespoons vinegar
	Tabasco sauce to taste
1	(6-ounce) can tomato paste

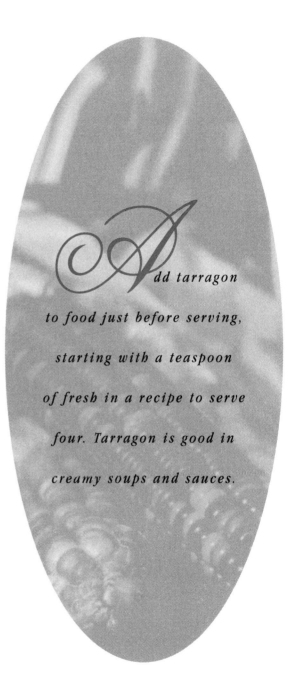

*A*dd tarragon to food just before serving, starting with a teaspoon of fresh in a recipe to serve four. Tarragon is good in creamy soups and sauces.

Rinse the chicken. Combine the chicken, salt pork and enough water to cover in a stockpot. Simmer for 45 to 60 minutes or until the chicken is tender; drain, reserving stock. Discard the salt pork. Remove skin and bones from chicken. Chop the chicken into bite-size pieces; place in a stockpot. Add 2 cups of the reserved stock.

Mash the drained tomatoes; add to the stock. Bring to a boil. Add corn, lima beans, salt, pepper, tarragon, basil, Worcestershire sauce, sugar, vinegar and Tabasco sauce. Simmer for 30 minutes over low heat, stirring occasionally. Stir in tomato paste. Simmer for 2 hours, stirring occasionally. Add additional reserved stock if needed.

yields eight servings

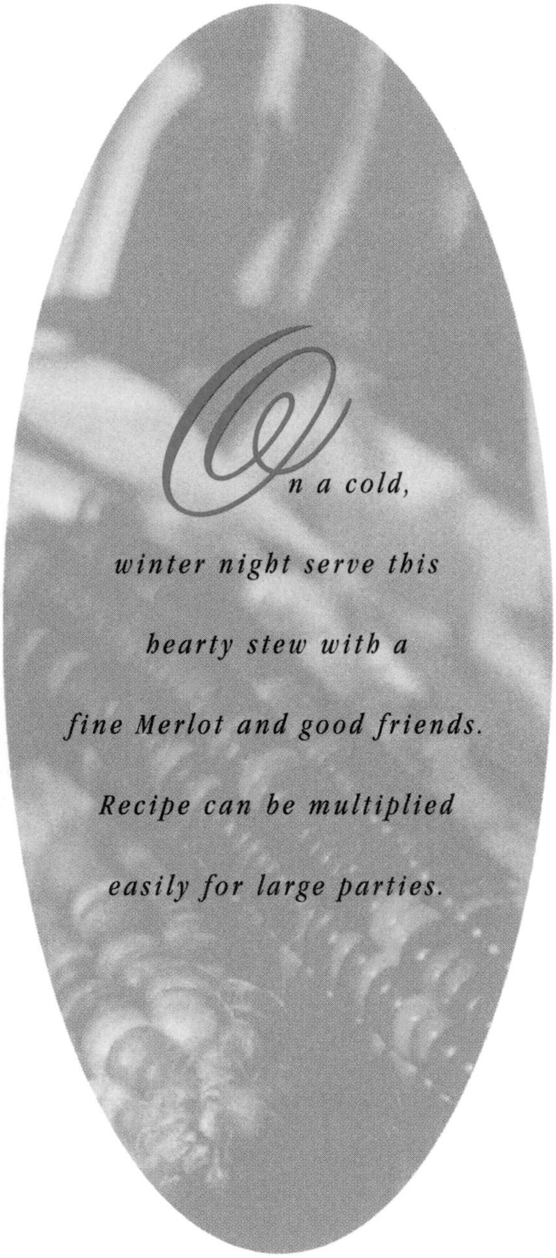

Harvest Hues

Lamb Stew

Ingredients

3	pounds lean lamb
4	large carrots, peeled
2	large onions
3	green bell peppers
1	(20-ounce) can tomatoes
	Salt and freshly ground pepper to taste

Trim all visible fat from the lamb; cut into 1½-inch cubes. Place lamb on rack in broiler pan. Cut carrots into 1-inch slices. Cut onions into ¼-inch slices; cut green peppers into ¼-inch strips.

Brown lamb quickly under hot broiler, turning to brown all sides. Combine lamb, carrots, onions, green peppers, tomatoes, salt and pepper in a stockpot. Simmer, covered, over low heat for 1 hour or until lamb is tender, stirring occasionally. Skim fat from top. Prepare lamb stew 1 day ahead if possible to allow flavors to blend.

yields six servings

On a cold, winter night serve this hearty stew with a fine Merlot and good friends. Recipe can be multiplied easily for large parties.

Veal Stew Provençale

Ingredients

2	pounds deboned veal shoulder
5	tablespoons flour
3	tablespoons vegetable oil
1	teaspoon salt
3	tablespoons Dijon mustard
1½	cups tomato juice
1½	cups white wine
12	peeled small carrots, cut lengthwise into quarters
12	small white onions
8	ounces fresh mushrooms, sliced

Enhanced by Italian Chianti or Sangieovese.

✑ Cut veal into 2-inch cubes. Sprinkle with flour, reserving any remaining flour. Brown the veal for 15 to 20 minutes in hot vegetable oil in a skillet, turning to brown all sides. Remove the veal to a greased 4-quart casserole. Stir the salt, mustard and reserved flour into the pan drippings. Add tomato juice and white wine gradually, stirring constantly. Pour over the veal.

✑ Bake, covered, at 350 degrees for 1 hour. Add the carrots and onions. Bake for 45 minutes.

✑ Add the mushrooms. Bake, covered, for 15 minutes or until the vegetables are tender. Stir the stew briefly to bring veal to top before serving.

yields six servings

Tailgating

Baked Brie with Elephant Garlic

Sausage Cheese Puffs

Tennessee Caviar

Big "O" Pretzels

Black-Eyed Bean Salad

Chicken Salad Galore

Corn Bread Salad

Marinated Green Beans

Grilled Marinated Flank Steak

Fried Chicken

Ham Sandwiches

Reuben Loaf

Chocolate Truffles

Touchdown Brownies

Cracker Candy

Orange Wassail

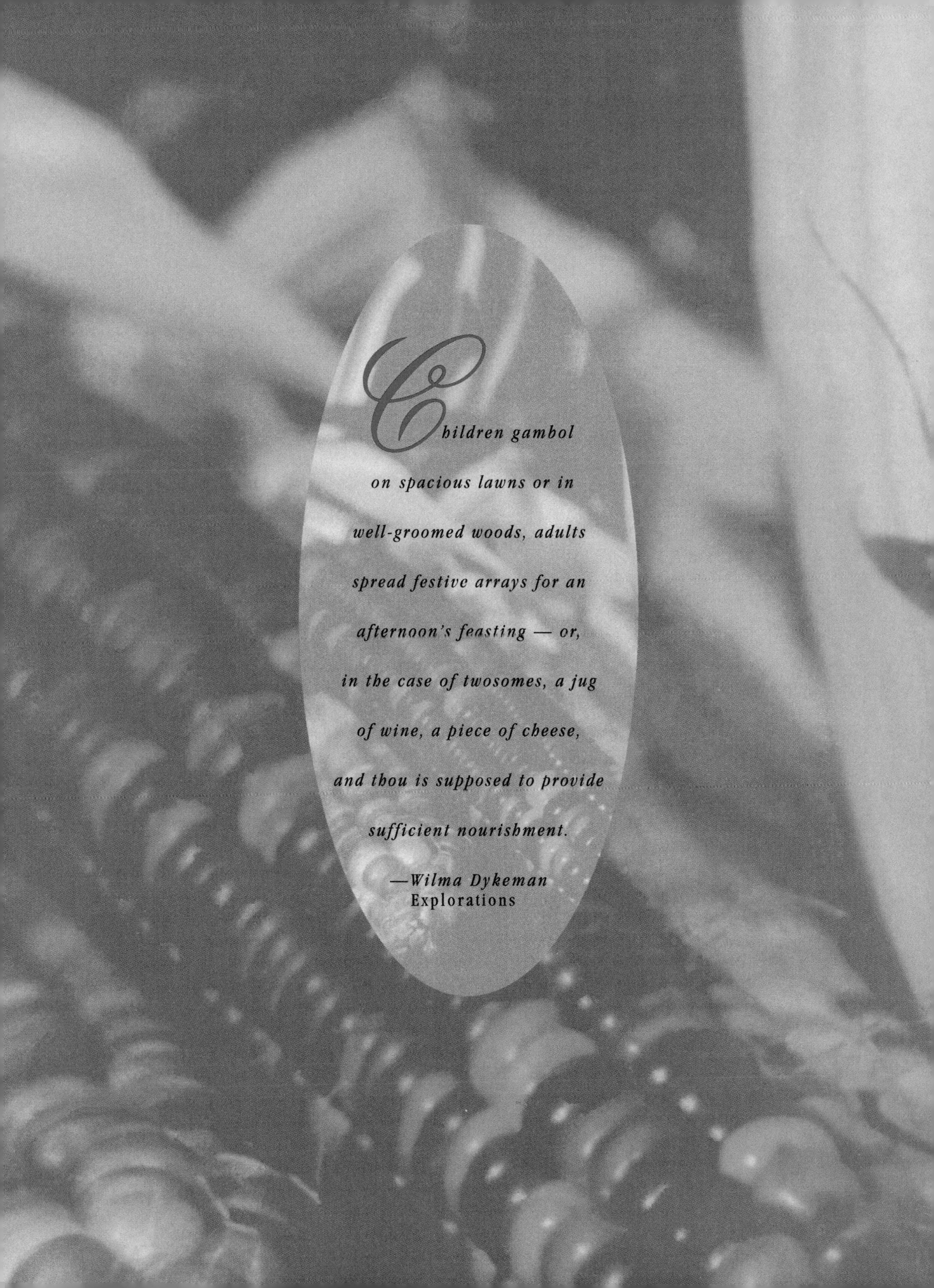

*C*hildren gambol

on spacious lawns or in

well-groomed woods, adults

spread festive arrays for an

afternoon's feasting — or,

in the case of twosomes, a jug

of wine, a piece of cheese,

and thou is supposed to provide

sufficient nourishment.

—*Wilma Dykeman*
Explorations

Harvest Hues

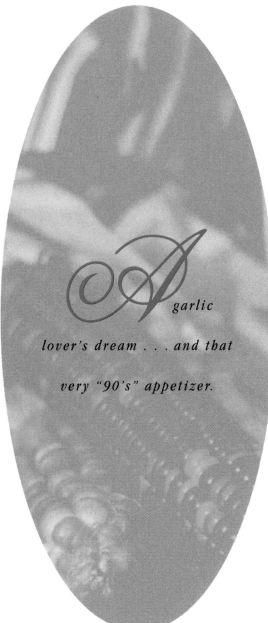

A garlic

lover's dream . . . and that

very "90's" appetizer.

Baked Brie with Elephant Garlic

Ingredients

 1 head elephant garlic
 2 tablespoons olive oil
 Salt and pepper to taste
 1 baguette, sliced
 4 ounces Brie cheese, warmed
 Sections of 2 oranges

Remove the papery exterior peel of garlic, leaving the bulb intact. Brush the garlic bulb with olive oil; sprinkle with salt and pepper. Place in a baking dish.

Bake at 350 degrees for 1 hour.

Place the bread slices on a baking sheet. Bake for 5 to 10 minutes or until toasted.

Arrange the garlic and warm cheese on a serving platter; surround with bread slices and orange sections. Serve by spreading the cheese on the bread and squeezing and spreading 1 garlic clove evenly over the cheese. Cleanse the palate with orange sections.

yields ten servings

Sausage Cheese Puffs

Ingredients

1	pound hot bulk sausage
2	cups sifted flour
1	teaspoon salt
⅔	cup margarine
5	(to 7) tablespoons cold water
½	cup cornmeal
½	cup shredded Monterey Jack jalapeño cheese

Brown the sausage in a skillet over medium heat, stirring until crumbly; drain. Chill, covered, in refrigerator.

Sift the flour and salt together into a bowl. Cut in the margarine until crumbly. Stir in the cold water 1 tablespoon at a time until the mixture is moist. Divide the dough into 4 portions. Flatten each portion of dough on a lightly floured surface. Remove to a cornmeal-coated surface. Roll the dough ⅛ inch thick. Cut into 3-inch squares.

Spoon 1 teaspoon of the sausage and ½ teaspoon of the cheese on each square. Fold the corners to the center, allowing the edges to overlap slightly. Place seam side down in a greased baking pan.

Bake at 400 degrees for 12 to 15 minutes or until lightly browned.

May freeze unbaked puffs for up to 3 months.

yields forty-eight appetizers

Bring

along a bottle of

California Zinfandel.

Harvest Hues

Tennessee Caviar

Ingredients

1	(15-ounce) can fresh shelled black-eyed peas, drained
1	(11-ounce) can Shoe Peg corn, drained
2	medium tomatoes, seeded, chopped
1	medium green bell pepper, finely chopped
2	(to 4) green onions, sliced
¼	(to ⅓) cup chopped fresh cilantro
1	cup picante sauce
2	tablespoons cider vinegar
2	cloves of garlic, minced

Combine the peas, corn, tomatoes, green pepper, green onions, cilantro, picante sauce, vinegar and garlic in a bowl; mix gently.

Chill in refrigerator for 8 hours or longer; drain. Serve with tortilla chips.

yields seven cups

Big "O" Pretzels

Ingredients

2	cups flour
1	envelope active dry yeast
4	pinches of salt
2	teaspoons sugar
¾	cup warm water
1	egg white
	Kosher salt to taste

Combine the flour, yeast, salt, sugar and water in a bowl. Mix until a light dough is formed. Knead the mixture lightly on a floured surface. Roll into large circles or other desired shapes. Place on a greased baking sheet. Mix the egg white with a small amount of water and brush over the dough. Sprinkle with kosher salt.

Bake at 425 degrees for 15 minutes.

yields six servings

Black-Eyed Bean Salad

Ingredients

1	cup instant rice
1	(10-ounce) package frozen baby lima beans
3	(15-ounce) cans black-eyed peas, drained, rinsed
1	medium red bell pepper, chopped
3	tablespoons chopped fresh parsley
2	tablespoons fresh squeezed lemon juice
2	tablespoons extra-virgin olive oil
1	tablespoon Dijon mustard
1	teaspoon sugar
	Salt and freshly ground pepper to taste

Cook the rice using package directions; cool. Cook the lima beans using package directions; drain.

Combine the rice, lima beans, peas, red pepper, parsley, lemon juice, olive oil, mustard, sugar, salt and pepper in a large bowl; mix well. Serve at room temperature.

yields ten servings

Brightly colored cloths, dishes and baskets of flowers combine for an inviting and casual backdrop to your tailgate event.

Harvest Hues

Chicken Salad Galore

Ingredients

2½	cups mayonnaise
½	cup sour cream
1	tablespoon curry powder
3	cups cold cooked rice
5	cups chopped cooked chicken breasts
1½	cups chopped green bell pepper
3	cups chopped celery
¾	cup seedless raisins
1¼	cups slivered almonds
3	(11-ounce) cans mandarin oranges, drained
2	(8-ounce) cans sliced water chestnuts, drained
	Salt and pepper to taste

Combine the mayonnaise, sour cream and curry powder in a large bowl; mix well. Add the rice, chicken, green pepper, celery, raisins, almonds, mandarin oranges, water chestnuts, salt and pepper; toss to mix well.

Spoon into a serving bowl.

yields twenty servings

Corn Bread Salad

Ingredients

1	(6-ounce) package corn bread mix
1	(4-ounce) can chopped green chiles, drained
	Pinch of sage
3	large tomatoes, chopped
½	cup chopped green bell pepper
½	cup chopped green onions
1	(1-ounce) package ranch salad dressing mix
1	cup sour cream
1	cup mayonnaise
2	(15-ounce) cans pinto beans, drained
2	cups shredded Cheddar cheese
10	slices crisp-cooked bacon, crumbled
2	(17-ounce) cans whole kernel golden sweet corn, drained

Prepare the corn bread mix with green chiles and sage using package directions for a 9-inch baking pan; cool slightly and crumble.

Mix the tomatoes, green pepper and green onions in a bowl. Mix the salad dressing mix, sour cream and mayonnaise in a bowl.

Layer corn bread crumbs, pinto beans, tomato mixture, cheese, bacon, corn and salad dressing ½ at a time in a large salad bowl. Chill, covered, in refrigerator for 2 to 3 hours before serving.

yields twelve servings

*G*reat side dish

for fried chicken at

your next tailgate party.

Marinated Green Beans

Ingredients

1½	pounds fresh green beans
8	slices bacon
6	tablespoons sugar
6	tablespoons vinegar
1	medium onion, cut into rings
½	cup slivered almonds

Trim the green beans; place in a steamer. Cook just until tender-crisp. Cook the bacon in a skillet until crisp; drain, reserving 3 tablespoons bacon drippings.

Combine the sugar, vinegar and reserved bacon drippings in a skillet. Heat just until the sugar is dissolved, stirring frequently.

Layer the green beans, onion rings and crumbled bacon in a greased 2-quart casserole. Pour the sugar mixture over layers; sprinkle the almonds on top.

Marinate, covered, in refrigerator for 8 to 12 hours.

Bake at 350 degrees for 45 minutes.

yields six servings

Grilled Marinated Flank Steak

Ingredients

1½	cups beer
4	scallions, minced
⅓	cup vegetable oil
3	tablespoons soy sauce
2	tablespoons light brown sugar
1	tablespoon minced peeled gingerroot
2	cloves of garlic, minced
1	teaspoon salt
1	teaspoon red pepper flakes
1¾	pounds flank steak

Combine the beer, scallions, oil, soy sauce, brown sugar, gingerroot, garlic, salt and red pepper in a bowl; mix well. Place the steak in a shallow dish; pour the marinade over the steak.

Marinate, covered, in refrigerator for 8 hours to 3 days, turning occasionally. Drain the steak and pat dry.

Grill the steak over hot coals or broil 2 inches from heat source for 5 minutes on each side for medium-rare or until done to taste. Cool slightly; cut diagonally cross grain into very thin slices.

yields six servings

Harvest Hues

F orget the diet . . .

everybody loves this southern

fried chicken!

Fried Chicken

Ingredients

1	(3-pound) chicken, cut up
2	cups milk
2½	cups flour
3	(to 4) tablespoons salt
1½	tablespoons pepper
	Oregano, basil and garlic to taste
	Vegetable oil for frying

Rinse the chicken; pat dry. Soak the chicken in milk in a bowl for 30 minutes. Combine the flour, salt, pepper, oregano, basil and garlic in a bowl; mix well. Remove the chicken from the milk; roll in the flour mixture to coat.

Fry the chicken in ¼ inch hot oil in a skillet until tender and golden brown, turning to brown both sides.

yields four servings

Ham Sandwiches

Ingredients

½	cup butter
8	onion rolls or hamburger buns, split
1	small onion, chopped
2	tablespoons poppy seeds
1	teaspoon dry mustard
1	pound shaved ham
8	ounces Swiss cheese, sliced

Spread the butter on cut sides of rolls, reserving 1 tablespoon butter. Sauté the onion in the reserved butter in a skillet until clear. Add the poppy seeds and dry mustard; mix well. Remove from heat. Layer the ham, a cheese slice and some of the onion mixture on half of each roll. Replace roll tops; wrap in foil. Place on a baking sheet.

Bake at 350 degrees for 20 minutes.

yields eight servings

Reuben Loaf

Ingredients

3¼	cups all-purpose flour
1	tablespoon sugar
1	teaspoon salt
1	envelope active dry yeast
1	cup hot water
1	tablespoon margarine, softened
¼	cup (or less) Dijon mustard
1	(6-ounce) jar sliced corned beef
1	(8-ounce) can sauerkraut, drained
4	slices Swiss cheese
1	egg white, beaten

Combine 2¼ cups of the flour with sugar, salt and yeast in a bowl; mix well. Stir in the hot water, margarine and enough of the remaining flour to make a soft dough. Knead for 4 minutes on a lightly floured surface. Roll the dough into a 10x14-inch rectangle. Place on a lightly greased baking sheet.

Spread the mustard lengthwise over half of the rolled dough. Layer the corned beef, sauerkraut and cheese in the order listed over the mustard. Fold the other half of the dough over the filling; seal the edges. Brush the top with beaten egg white. Cut slits in the top of the dough.

Bake at 400 degrees for 25 to 30 minutes or until golden brown. Cut into slices to serve.

yields six servings

Fall mums, rovers, spiker mums, garnet kings and golden aster in a hollowed-out pumpkin make a traditional fall-colored, casual arrangement.

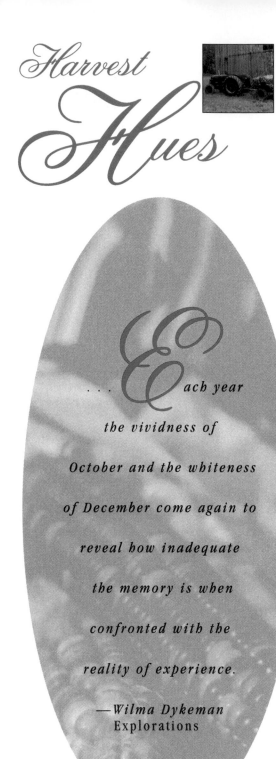

Chocolate Truffles

Ingredients

1	(16-ounce) package vanilla wafers
1	egg, lightly beaten
2	tablespoons vanilla extract
1	cup melted margarine
1	cup chopped walnuts
¼	cup European-processed baking cocoa
2	tablespoons Cognac
½	(1-pound) package confectioners' sugar
1¼	cups dark jersey cocoa

Crush the wafers in a food processor until crumbly. Combine with next 7 ingredients in a bowl; mix well.

Shape into bite-sized balls and roll in dark jersey cocoa. Place in small cupcake liners. Chill, covered, in an airtight container. Remove from refrigerator 1 hour before serving.

yields sixty truffles

Touchdown Brownies

Ingredients

½	cup butter
4	ounces unsweetened chocolate
1½	teaspoons vanilla extract
1¾	cups sugar
2	eggs
1	cup flour
1	cup chopped pecans

Melt the butter in a saucepan over very low heat. Stir in the chocolate until melted. Let stand for 10 minutes. Add the vanilla. Stir in the sugar gradually until mixed. Add the eggs 1 at a time, beating well after each addition. Stir in the flour and pecans gradually. Spoon into a greased and floured 9x9-inch baking pan.

Bake at 350 degrees for 30 minutes.

yields sixteen servings

Cracker Candy

Ingredients

40	saltines
1	cup butter
1	cup packed light brown sugar
2	cups milk chocolate chips

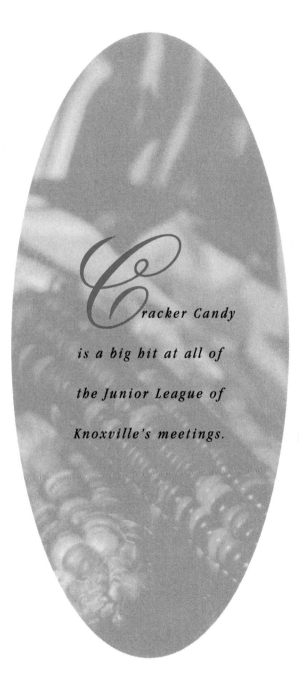

*C**racker Candy is a big hit at all of the Junior League of Knoxville's meetings.*

❧ Place the crackers side by side in a foil-lined baking pan. Combine the butter and brown sugar in a saucepan. Bring to a boil. Cook for 3 minutes, stirring constantly. Spread the mixture over the crackers.

❧ Bake at 400 degrees for 5 minutes. Sprinkle chocolate chips over baked crackers. Let stand for 5 minutes; spread the melted chocolate over the top.

❧ Chill in refrigerator until firm. Invert onto a flat surface; remove foil. Break into pieces. Store, covered, in an airtight container in refrigerator.

yields twenty-four candies

Orange Wassail

Ingredients

1	cup water
12	whole cloves
2	cinnamon sticks
4	cups cranberry juice cocktail
12	cups orange juice

❧ Bring the water to a boil in a large saucepan. Add the cloves and cinnamon. Boil for 2 minutes.

❧ Stir in the cranberry juice cocktail and orange juice.

❧ Simmer for 10 minutes. Keep warm until serving time.

yields seventeen cups

Tones of Winter

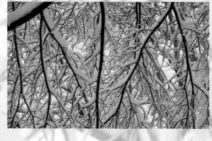

BEVERAGES

DESSERTS

*S*now's revelations

are as tiny as the tracery

of a bird track on the

windowsill and as majestic as

the sculpted slope of a

pinnacle on the distant horizon.

The scrawled blackness of

an elm branch becomes a

masterpiece of design outlined

with a frosting of snow.

—Wilma Dykeman
Explorations

Beverages

Perhaps one of the most compelling experiences indicating this love of place concerned a Middle Tennessee boy who once complained, in the presence of his grandfather, of muddy drinking water and was sharply reprimanded: "Remember, you're drinking the sacred soil of your native land!"

—Wilma Dykeman
Tennessee,
A History

*I*mages of rolling

greens, expansive front porches,

rocking chairs and steamy,

southern summer nights . . . a glass

of iced tea on the front porch is a

well known southern image . . . an

open invitation for entertaining

close friends and the regular

neighbor who "comes a-calling."

Serve the tea hot

in the winter.

Fruit Tea

Ingredients

1	quart water
7	regular tea bags
1	cup (or less) sugar
1	(6-ounce) can frozen orange juice
1	(6-ounce) can frozen lemonade

Bring the water to a boil in a saucepan. Pour over the tea bags in a bowl; let steep for 5 minutes. Remove tea bags. Add the sugar, stirring until dissolved. Stir in orange juice and lemonade until thawed and well mixed.

Pour mixture into a 1-gallon container. Add enough cold water to fill the container. Serve over ice. Garnish with lemon slices or mint leaves.

yields one gallon

Ginger Tea

Ingredients

3	tablespoons (heaping) instant tea
1½	cups sugar
2	cups orange juice
1	(6-ounce) can frozen limeade concentrate, thawed
6	cups water
1	quart ginger ale, chilled

Combine tea, sugar, orange juice, limeade concentrate and water in a large container; mix well. Chill, covered, until serving time.

Pour in ginger ale just before serving.

yields one gallon

Plantation Almond Tea

Ingredients

2	cups boiling water
2	tea bags
½	cup sugar
¼	cup lemon juice
1	teaspoon almond extract
1	teaspoon vanilla extract
2	cups ice water

Pour the boiling water over the tea bags in a large container. Let steep for 10 minutes; remove tea bags. Add sugar, stirring until dissolved. Add lemon juice, flavorings and ice water; mix well. Serve over ice. Garnish with an orange slice and a cherry.

yields four and one-half cups

Holiday Wassail

Ingredients

2	quarts apple cider
2	cups orange juice
1	cup lemon juice
5	cups pineapple juice
¼	cup honey
1	cinnamon stick
2	teaspoons whole cloves
1	orange, sliced
1	(7-ounce) package red hot cinnamon candies

Combine the apple cider, orange juice, lemon juice, pineapple juice, honey, cinnamon stick, cloves, orange slices and red hot cinnamon candies in a large saucepan.

Simmer, covered, over low heat for 1½ hours, stirring occasionally. Strain before serving. Garnish with additional orange slices.

yields one gallon

Tones of Winter

Capture the Christmas Spirit in its purity . . . with snow, white lights, red decorations, candles everywhere and a small glass of this spirit-warming beverage served in the evening before dinner.

Hot Swedish Vinglögg

Ingredients

1	bottle sweet red wine
½	bottle madeira
1	tablespoon whole cardamom seeds
1	(to 2) cinnamon sticks
¼	cup packed light brown sugar
	Peel of ½ lemon, thinly sliced
3	tablespoons raisins
3	tablespoons chopped almonds

Combine the wines, cardamom seeds and cinnamon sticks in a large saucepan. Heat over medium-low heat; do not boil. Add the brown sugar, stirring until dissolved. Add the lemon. Heat for 10 to 15 minutes, stirring occasionally and lowering the heat if necessary to prevent boiling.

Mix the raisins and almonds in a bowl. Spoon 1 to 2 tablespoons into a mug or cup. Add the wine mixture. Add a small spoon to the mug to scoop up raisins and almonds.

yields six servings

Cappuccino Mix

Ingredients

3½	cups nonfat dry milk powder
2½	cups sugar
1½	cups instant coffee
½	cup baking cocoa
1	teaspoon cinnamon

Combine the dry milk powder, sugar, coffee powder, baking cocoa and cinnamon in a bowl; mix well. Store in an airtight container. Stir 1 heaping tablespoonful into 6 ounces hot water to serve. May add a dollop of whipped topping if desired.

yields eighty-five servings

Spice Mix for Mulled Beverage

Ingredients

	Peel of 2 oranges, cut into ½-inch strips
8	cinnamon sticks
¼	cup whole cloves
¼	cup whole allspice
4	whole nutmegs, broken
3	drops oil of cinnamon

Place the orange peel outer side up on a wire rack on a baking sheet.

Bake at 200 degrees with the oven door slightly ajar for 2 to 2½ hours or until the orange peel is dry, checking frequently. Cool. Break the peel into small pieces in a bowl. Break cinnamon sticks into small pieces; add to orange peel. Add cloves, allspice and nutmegs. Add oil of cinnamon; mix well. Tie mixture into cheesecloth bags in ⅓-cup portions. Combine each spice bag with ½ gallon of a beverage such as wine or apple cider in a saucepan. Bring to a boil. Reduce the heat. Simmer for 30 minutes; remove the spice bag. Serve warm.

May use loose spices in beverage and strain before serving.

yields one and one-third cups

Tones of Winter

Freeze a circular mold filled with a mixture of the base ingredients in the punch—orange juice, lemonade, cranberry juice, whatever—and adorn with mint sprigs, pansies or fruit slices. Place in punch to keep it chilled without watering down the taste.

Crimson Punch

Ingredients

½	cup sugar
1	cup boiling water
2	pints cranberry juice
1	pint orange juice
½	cup lemon juice
2	fifths white Champagne or 4 (7-ounce) bottles ginger ale

Add the sugar to the boiling water in a saucepan, stirring until the sugar dissolves. Add the cranberry juice, orange juice and lemon juice. Pour into a large container. Chill, covered, in refrigerator until very cold. Add Champagne or ginger ale just before serving.

yields thirty (four-ounce) servings

Slush Punch

Ingredients

4	cups sugar
1	(3-ounce) package red gelatin
3	cups boiling water
3	cups cold water
5	bananas
1	(12-ounce) can frozen orange juice concentrate, thawed
1	(12-ounce) can frozen lemonade concentrate, thawed
1	(48-ounce) can pineapple juice, chilled
2	gallons ginger ale, chilled

Mix the sugar and gelatin in a bowl. Add the boiling water, stirring until the mixture dissolves. Stir in the cold water. Chill in refrigerator.

Place bananas in a blender container; process until puréed. Add the bananas, orange juice and lemonade concentrates and pineapple juice to the gelatin mixture. Pour into a freezer container; mix well. Freeze, covered, just until slushy. Add an equal amount of ginger ale just before serving.

yields four gallons

Sparkling Champagne Punch

Ingredients

2	cups cranberry juice cocktail
2	cups orange juice
¼	cup lemon juice
½	cup sugar
1½	cups white wine, chilled
1	bottle Champagne, chilled

Combine the cranberry juice cocktail, orange juice, lemon juice and sugar in a bowl, stirring until the sugar dissolves. Chill in refrigerator.

Pour into a punch bowl. Add the wine and Champagne just before serving. Garnish with orange slices.

yields two and one-fourth quarts

White Christmas Punch

Ingredients

2	cups sugar
1	cup water
1	(12-ounce) can evaporated milk
1	tablespoon almond extract
3	(½-gallon) cartons vanilla ice cream
6	(2-liter) bottles lemon-lime carbonated beverage, chilled

Combine the sugar and water in a saucepan. Cook over medium heat until the sugar dissolves, stirring constantly. Remove from the heat. Stir in the evaporated milk and almond flavoring. Chill until serving time.

Combine the evaporated milk mixture, ice cream and carbonated beverage in a punch bowl, stirring to break the ice cream into small pieces.

yields three and one-half gallons

Tones of Winter

*F*ill a holiday mug with a decorative bag of your hot drink mix and include the recipe.

Minted Hot Cocoa

Ingredients

3	(4-inch) peppermint candy sticks
1	cup powdered nondairy creamer
1	cup sifted confectioners' sugar
¼	cup baking cocoa

❧ Crush the candy sticks with a mallet. Combine the candy, nondairy creamer, confectioners' sugar and baking cocoa in a bowl; mix well. Store in a covered container.

❧ Combine ¼ cup of the mixture with ¾ cup boiling water to serve. May add ½ cup instant coffee powder to mixture for mocha flavor.

yields three cups

Irish Cream Liqueur

Ingredients

1½	cups Irish whiskey
1	(14-ounce) can sweetened condensed milk
2	cups whipping cream
2	tablespoons chocolate syrup
2	teaspoons instant coffee
3	teaspoons vanilla extract
½	teaspoon almond extract

❧ Combine the whiskey, condensed milk, whipping cream, chocolate syrup, instant coffee powder, vanilla and almond flavorings in blender container; process until smooth.

❧ Store in covered container in refrigerator for up to 1 month. Stir well just before serving; pour into liqueur glasses.

yields approximately five cups

The Perfect Oyster Shooter

Ingredients

1	fifth high-grade vodka
12	fresh whole oysters, shucked, cleaned
¾	cup spicy cocktail sauce

Place vodka in freezer for 8 to 10 hours. Place 1 oyster in each shot glass. Cover with vodka. Add a large dollop of cocktail sauce.

Shots are traditionally drunk in one fast gulp; chewing the oyster is a personal choice.

yields twelve servings

The Quintessential Bloody Mary

Ingredients

10	ounces tomato juice or vegetable juice cocktail
2	ounces vodka
1	tablespoon fresh lime juice
½	teaspoon celery salt
½	teaspoon freshly ground pepper
½	teaspoon salt
⅓	teaspoon horseradish
	Worcestershire sauce to taste

Combine tomato juice, vodka, lime juice, celery salt, pepper, salt, horseradish and Worcestershire sauce in a bowl; mix well.

Pour over shaved ice in a tall glass. Garnish with celery or a slice of cucumber. May substitute soda water for vodka.

yields one serving

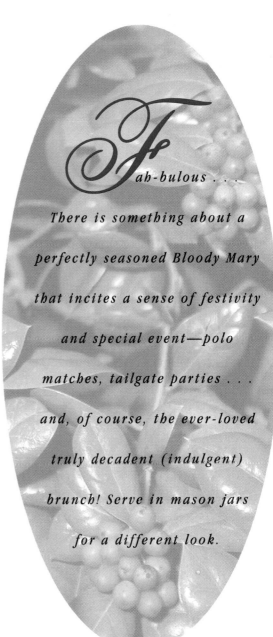

*F*ab-bulous . . .

There is something about a
perfectly seasoned Bloody Mary
that incites a sense of festivity
and special event—polo
matches, tailgate parties . . .
and, of course, the ever-loved
truly decadent (indulgent)
brunch! Serve in mason jars
for a different look.

Desserts

Cream Puffs

Lemon Cream Freeze

Chocolate Amaretto Cheesecake

Luscious Cheesecake

Black Forest Cake

Blackstone Chocolate Satin Cake

Carrot Cake

Fresh Apple Cake

Caramel Applesauce Cake

Coca-Cola Cake

Holiday Cake

Hummingbird Cake

Chocolate Sour Cream Pound Cake

Cream Cheese Pound Cake

Lavender Pound Cake

Apple Sheet Pie

Buttermilk Pie

Peaches-and-Cream Pie

Strawberry Chiffon Pie

Coconut Caramel Pies

Fresh Fruit Tart

Pear Almond Tart

Tennessee Pecan Pie

Blackberry Cobbler

"Out-of-This-League" Brownies

Date-Nut Bars

Ginger Cookies

Lemon Sugar Cookies

Holiday Shortbread

Chocolate Almond Biscotti

*T*here are

"appetizer" people

and "dessert" people . . .

those who await the

delights of the sweets

may never discover

the delectability of

the appetizer.

—*Wilma Dykeman*
Explorations

For a French alternative, fill puffs with good vanilla ice cream and cover generously with hot fudge before serving.

Cream Puffs

Ingredients

1	cup water
½	cup margarine
½	teaspoon salt
1	cup flour
4	eggs
6	tablespoons flour
¼	cup sugar
¼	teaspoon salt
2	cups milk, scalded
2	eggs
¼	cup sugar
1	tablespoon butter
1	teaspoon vanilla extract
1	cup whipping cream, whipped
	Fudge Sauce

Bring the water and margarine to a boil in a saucepan over medium heat. Stir in a mixture of ½ teaspoon salt and 1 cup flour all at once. Cook over low heat until mixture leaves side of pan and forms a smooth ball, stirring constantly. Add 4 eggs 1 at a time, beating with a wooden spoon. Drop the batter by heaping tablespoonfuls 3 inches apart onto a nonstick baking sheet.

Bake at 425 degrees for 10 minutes. Reduce the oven temperature to 350 degrees.

Bake for 25 minutes, covering with foil if cream puff shells are browning too rapidly. Cool. Cut off tops; remove soft dough inside.

Combine 6 tablespoons flour, ¼ cup sugar and ¼ teaspoon salt in a double boiler. Stir in scalded milk. Cook over boiling water for 10 minutes or until thickened, stirring constantly.

Beat 2 eggs and ¼ cup sugar in a bowl. Stir a small amount of the hot mixture into the beaten eggs; stir eggs into hot mixture. Cook for 5 minutes longer, stirring constantly. Stir in the butter. Cool. Stir in the vanilla. Chill, covered, in refrigerator. Fold in whipped cream.

Fill the cream puffs with custard filling; replace tops. Drizzle with the Fudge Sauce. Store in refrigerator.

Fudge Sauce

Ingredients

1	(2-ounce) square unsweetened chocolate
2	tablespoons light corn syrup
2	tablespoons butter
1	cup sugar
½	cup evaporated milk, warmed
½	teaspoon vanilla extract

Combine the chocolate, corn syrup and butter in a double boiler. Cook over boiling water until the chocolate and butter are melted, stirring frequently. Add the sugar; mix well. Add the warm evaporated milk. Cook for 15 to 20 minutes or until thickened, stirring constantly. Stir in the vanilla. Remove from the heat. Sauce will thicken slightly as it stands. Fudge Sauce may be stored, covered, in refrigerator.

yields twelve servings

Lemon Cream Freeze

Ingredients

	Juice of 2 lemons
1¾	cups sugar
¼	teaspoon vanilla extract
¼	teaspoon salt
2½	cups whipping cream, whipped
	Grated peel of 2 lemons

Combine the lemon juice and sugar in a bowl; mix well. Chill, covered, in refrigerator for 8 to 10 hours. Stir in the vanilla and salt. Fold in the whipped cream and grated lemon peel.

Spoon into a 7x11-inch dish. Cover with plastic or foil. Store in freezer for 8 to 10 hours.

yields eight servings

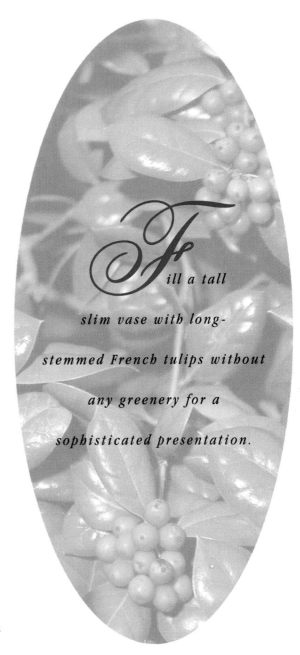

Fill a tall slim vase with long-stemmed French tulips without any greenery for a sophisticated presentation.

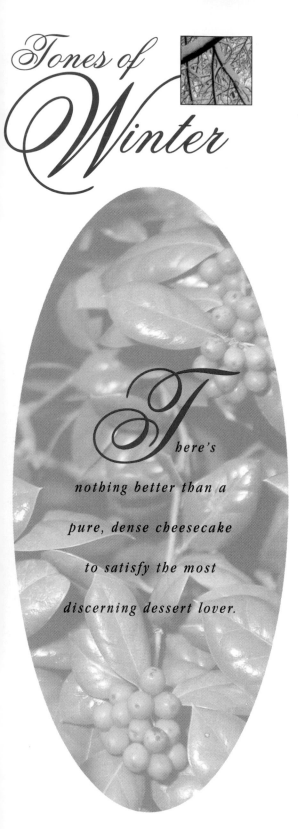

Tones of Winter

There's nothing better than a pure, dense cheesecake to satisfy the most discerning dessert lover.

Chocolate Amaretto Cheesecake

Ingredients

1½	cups graham cracker crumbs
6	tablespoons melted butter
¼	cup sugar
24	ounces cream cheese, softened
⅔	cup confectioners' sugar
4	large eggs
5	ounces milk chocolate, melted
½	cup amaretto
¼	cup melted butter
1	cup sour cream

Combine graham cracker crumbs, 6 tablespoons melted butter and sugar in a bowl; mix well. Press onto bottom and up side of a buttered 9-inch springform pan.

Bake at 350 degrees for 10 minutes.

Combine the cream cheese and confectioners' sugar in a mixer bowl; beat until creamy. Add eggs 1 at a time, beating well after each addition. Add melted chocolate, amaretto, ¼ cup melted butter and sour cream; mix until blended. Spoon into graham cracker crust.

Bake at 350 degrees for 45 to 60 minutes or until center is almost set. Turn off the oven. Let cheesecake stand in the oven with door open until cooled to room temperature. Chill in refrigerator.

yields eight servings

Luscious Cheesecake

Ingredients

1½	cups graham cracker crumbs
¼	cup sugar
6	tablespoons melted butter
	Dash of cinnamon
24	ounces cream cheese, softened
1½	cups sugar
4	eggs
1	teaspoon vanilla extract
2	cups sour cream
¼	cup sugar
2	teaspoons vanilla extract

Combine the graham cracker crumbs, ¼ cup sugar, butter and cinnamon in a bowl; mix well. Press onto bottom and up side of a buttered 9-inch springform pan. Chill in refrigerator.

Beat cream cheese and 1½ cups sugar in mixer bowl until well mixed. Add eggs 1 at a time, beating well after each addition. Add 1 teaspoon vanilla; mix well. Spoon into graham cracker crust.

Bake at 350 degrees for 1 hour. Let stand at room temperature for 15 minutes.

Combine sour cream, ¼ cup sugar and 2 teaspoons vanilla in mixer bowl; mix well. Spread over cheesecake.

Bake at 450 degrees for 10 minutes. Store in refrigerator.

yields twelve servings

Tones of Winter

Evergreens—

fir and pine spruce—mixed

with magnolias, holly branches

and red gerbera daisies

will adorn your table

in Christmas color.

Black Forest Cake

Ingredients

1	cup egg whites
	Pinch of cream of tartar
2	cups plus 2 tablespoons sugar
1	teaspoon vanilla extract
1	(4½-ounce) package slivered almonds, finely chopped
3	egg whites
¾	cup sugar
3	tablespoons baking cocoa
1	(4-ounce) bar German's sweet chocolate, grated
1½	cups butter, softened
	Whipped Cream Icing

Cut four 9-inch circles from parchment paper. Place on a baking pan; grease paper circles. Beat the 1 cup egg whites in a mixer bowl until foamy. Add cream of tartar; beat until soft peaks form. Add 2 cups plus 2 tablespoons sugar and vanilla, beating until stiff. Fold in almonds. Spread on each paper circle.

Bake at 225 degrees for 2½ hours. Turn off the oven. Let the meringues stand in the oven for 5 to 10 hours or until thoroughly dry.

Beat the 3 eggs whites in a double boiler over hot water until soft peaks form. Add the ¾ cup sugar and baking cocoa, beating until stiff. Reserve half of the grated chocolate. Fold in the butter and remaining grated chocolate. Chill until of spreading consistency. Spread over each meringue. Chill in refrigerator.

Spread Whipped Cream Icing between meringue layers and over top and side. Sprinkle the top with reserved grated chocolate. Store in refrigerator or freezer.

Whipped Cream Icing

Ingredients

4	cups whipping cream
3	tablespoons vanilla extract
⅓	cup sugar

Beat the whipping cream in a mixer bowl until soft peaks form. Add the vanilla and sugar, beating until stiff.

yields twelve servings

Blackstone Chocolate Satin Cake

Ingredients

8	ounces cream cheese, softened
½	cup sugar
5	large eggs
1	cup sugar
½	cup water
24	ounces semisweet chocolate, chopped
1	cup butter
1	cup whipping cream
	Raspberry Sauce

❧ Beat the cream cheese and ½ cup sugar in a mixer bowl for 4 minutes. Beat in the eggs 1 at a time. Combine 1 cup sugar and water in a saucepan. Bring to a boil, stirring occasionally. Stir in half the chocolate and butter until melted. Pour into the cream cheese mixture. Beat until smooth.

❧ Line a buttered 9-inch cake pan with buttered parchment or waxed paper. Spoon the batter into the prepared pan. Place the cake pan in a bain-marie.

❧ Bake at 375 degrees on the center rack of the oven for 1 hour or until the cake tests done. Cool in the pan for several minutes. Loosen the cake from the side of the pan with a knife. Invert onto a wire rack; remove the parchment.

❧ Heat the whipping cream to the boiling point in a saucepan. Stir in the remaining chocolate until melted and smooth. Drizzle over the cake. Serve with the Raspberry Sauce.

Raspberry Sauce

Ingredients

2	cups frozen or fresh raspberries
½	cup confectioners' sugar
	Juice of ½ lemon
¼	cup crème de cassis

❧ Combine the raspberries, confectioners' sugar and lemon juice in a saucepan. Simmer until thickened, stirring frequently.

❧ Strain to remove the seeds if desired. Stir in the crème de cassis.

yields sixteen servings

*T*his is one

way to get your kids

to eat carrots!

Carrot Cake

Ingredients

2	cups flour
1	teaspoon salt
1½	teaspoons baking powder
1½	teaspoons baking soda
2	teaspoons cinnamon
2	cups sugar
1¼	cups canola oil
1	cup egg substitute
2½	cups grated carrots
1	(8-ounce) can crushed pineapple, drained
2	teaspoons vanilla extract
	Light Cream Cheese Frosting

Combine the flour, salt, baking powder, baking soda and cinnamon in a bowl; mix well. Combine the sugar, oil and egg substitute in a bowl. Add to the dry ingredients. Stir in the carrots, pineapple and vanilla. Spoon into 2 greased and floured 8-inch round cake pans.

Bake at 350 degrees for 40 to 45 minutes or until the cake tests done. Cool in the pans for several minutes; remove to wire racks to cool completely. Spread the Light Cream Cheese Frosting between the layers and over top and side of cooled cake.

Light Cream Cheese Frosting

Ingredients

⅔	cup margarine, softened
11	ounces Neufchâtel cheese, softened
1½	(1-pound) packages confectioners' sugar
2	teaspoons vanilla extract

Beat the margarine and Neufchâtel cheese in a mixer bowl at low speed until blended. Add the confectioners' sugar gradually, beating at high speed until smooth and fluffy. Add the vanilla; beat well.

yields twelve servings

Fresh Apple Cake

Ingredients

2	cups sugar
1½	cups corn oil
3	eggs
3	cups flour
1	teaspoon baking soda
1	teaspoon salt
3	cups finely chopped Granny Smith apples
2½	cups chopped pecans
2	teaspoons vanilla extract
	Creamy Caramel Glaze

Combine the sugar and oil in a mixer bowl; beat well. Add the eggs 1 at a time, beating well after each addition. Add a mixture of flour, baking soda and salt gradually. Beat in the apples, pecans and vanilla. Spoon into a greased and floured 9-inch tube pan.

Bake at 325 degrees for 1¼ to 1½ hours or until the cake tests done. Do not overbake.

Pierce holes in the top of the hot cake with a wooden pick. Pour ⅓ of the warm Creamy Caramel Glaze over the hot cake. Cool in the pan for 10 minutes; invert onto a cake plate to cool for 20 minutes. Drizzle remaining Creamy Caramel Glaze over the cake. Creamy Caramel Glaze may be reheated if it becomes too thick to drizzle.

Creamy Caramel Glaze

Ingredients

1	cup packed dark brown sugar
½	cup butter
½	cup whipping cream

Combine the brown sugar, butter and whipping cream in a saucepan. Bring to a boil. Reduce the heat. Simmer for 3 minutes, stirring constantly.

yields sixteen servings

Caramel Applesauce Cake

Ingredients

½	cup butter, softened
1½	cups sugar
3	eggs
2	cups flour
2	teaspoons baking soda
	Pinch of salt
1	teaspoon cinnamon
½	teaspoon cloves
1½	cups applesauce
½	cup chopped dates
½	cup chopped pecans
	Fruit Nut Filling
	Caramel Frosting

Cream the butter and sugar in a mixer bowl until light and fluffy. Add the eggs 1 at a time, beating well after each addition. Mix 1¾ cups of the flour, baking soda, salt, cinnamon and cloves together. Add to the creamed mixture alternately with the applesauce, beginning and ending with the flour mixture. Coat the dates and pecans with the remaining ¼ cup flour. Fold into the batter. Spoon into 3 greased and floured 8-inch round cake pans.

Bake at 350 degrees for 25 to 30 minutes or until the cake tests done. Cool in pans for 10 minutes; remove to a wire rack to cool completely.

Spread Fruit Nut Filling between layers of the cooled cake. Spread Caramel Frosting over top and side of cake.

Fruit Nut Filling

Ingredients

- ¼   cup flour
- 2   tablespoons sugar
- ½   cup water
- ¼   cup butter
- ¼   cup plus 2 tablespoons chopped dates
- ¼   cup plus 2 tablespoons raisins
- ¼   cup chopped pecans

Combine the flour and sugar in a medium saucepan; mix well. Add the water gradually, mixing well. Stir in the butter, dates, raisins and pecans. Cook over medium heat until thickened, stirring constantly. Cool.

Caramel Frosting

- 1   cup butter
- 1   cup sugar
- 1   cup packed brown sugar
- 1   cup evaporated milk

Melt the butter in a heavy saucepan over medium heat. Add the sugar, brown sugar and evaporated milk. Cook over medium heat to 234 to 240 degrees on candy thermometer, soft-ball stage, stirring constantly. Remove from heat. Cool for 10 minutes. Beat at medium speed for 8 to 10 minutes or until of spreading consistency.

yields twelve servings

A crystal vase filled with white lilies, magnolia and holly is fragrant and beautiful.

Coca-Cola Cake

Ingredients

2	cups flour
2	cups sugar
1	cup butter
3	tablespoons baking cocoa
1	cup Coca-Cola
½	cup buttermilk
2	eggs, beaten
1	teaspoon baking soda
1	teaspoon vanilla extract
1½	(to 2½) cups miniature marshmallows
	Coca-Cola Icing

Combine the flour and sugar in a mixer bowl; mix well. Heat the butter, baking cocoa and Coca-Cola in a saucepan to the boiling point, stirring constantly. Pour into the flour mixture; beat well. Add the buttermilk, eggs, baking soda and vanilla; beat well. Stir in the marshmallows. Spoon into a greased and floured 9x11-inch cake pan.

Bake at 350 degrees for 30 to 40 minutes or until the cake tests done.

Spread Coca-Cola Icing over the hot cake.

Coca-Cola Icing

Ingredients

½	cup butter
3	tablespoons baking cocoa
6	tablespoons Coca-Cola
1	(1-pound) package confectioners' sugar
1	cup chopped pecans

Combine the butter, baking cocoa and Coca-Cola in a saucepan. Bring to a boil, stirring constantly. Pour over the confectioners' sugar in a mixer bowl; beat well. Fold in the pecans.

yields twelve servings

Holiday Cake

Ingredients

2½	cups self-rising flour
1	teaspoon baking soda
1½	cups sugar
1	teaspoon baking cocoa
2	large eggs
1	cup buttermilk
1½	cups vegetable oil
1	teaspoon vanilla extract
2	(1-ounce) bottles red food coloring
1	teaspoon white vinegar
	Nutty Cream Cheese Frosting
½	cup pecans

Combine the flour, baking soda, sugar and baking cocoa in a mixer bowl. Add the eggs 1 at a time, beating well after each addition. Add the buttermilk, oil, vanilla, food coloring and vinegar; beat well. Spoon the batter into three 9-inch cake pans sprayed with nonstick baking spray.

Bake at 350 degrees for 20 minutes or until the cake tests done. Cool in the pans for several minutes; remove to a wire rack to cool completely.

Spread Nutty Cream Cheese Frosting between layers and on top and side of the cooled cake. Sprinkle the pecans over the top. Chill in refrigerator for 1 hour before serving.

Nutty Cream Cheese Frosting

Ingredients

½	cup plus 2⅔ tablespoons butter, softened
10	ounces cream cheese, softened
1	(1-pound) package confectioners' sugar
1½	cups chopped pecans

Combine the butter and cream cheese in a mixer bowl; beat well. Add the confectioners' sugar; beat until creamy. Fold in pecans.

yields twelve servings

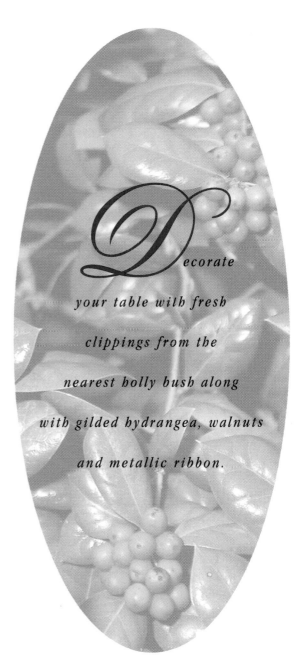

Decorate your table with fresh clippings from the nearest holly bush along with gilded hydrangea, walnuts and metallic ribbon.

Red and white striped carnations, evergreen and candy canes in small baskets wrapped in ribbon make a delightful table setting.

Hummingbird Cake

Ingredients

3	cups flour
2	cups sugar
1	teaspoon baking soda
1	teaspoon salt
1	teaspoon cinnamon
3	eggs, beaten
1	cup vegetable oil
1½	teaspoons vanilla extract
1	(8-ounce) can crushed pineapple
1	cup chopped pecans
2	cups chopped bananas
	Cream Cheese Frosting
½	cup chopped pecans

Combine the flour, sugar, baking soda, salt and cinnamon in a bowl; mix well. Stir in the eggs and oil just until the flour mixture is moistened. Stir in the vanilla, undrained pineapple, pecans and bananas. Spoon the batter into 3 greased and floured 9-inch round cake pans.

Bake at 350 degrees for 25 to 30 minutes or until the cake tests done. Cool in the pans for 10 minutes. Invert onto a wire rack to cool completely.

Spread Cream Cheese Frosting between layers and on top and side of cooled cake. Sprinkle the pecans on top.

Cream Cheese Frosting

Ingredients

8	ounces cream cheese, softened
½	cup butter, softened
1	(1-pound) package confectioners' sugar, sifted
1	teaspoon vanilla extract

Combine the cream cheese and butter in a mixer bowl; beat well. Add the confectioners' sugar and vanilla; beat until fluffy.

yields twelve servings

Chocolate Sour Cream Pound Cake

Ingredients

1½	cups margarine, softened
3	cups sugar
5	eggs
3	cups flour
½	cup baking cocoa
1	teaspoon baking soda
¼	teaspoon salt
1	cup sour cream
1	cup boiling water
2	teaspoons vanilla extract
	Creamy Chocolate Glaze

Cream the margarine and sugar in a mixer bowl until light and fluffy. Add eggs 1 at a time, beating well after each addition. Sift the flour, baking cocoa, baking soda and salt together. Add to the creamed mixture alternately with the sour cream, beginning and ending with the flour mixture. Beat well after each addition Add the boiling water and vanilla; beat well. Spoon the batter into a greased and floured bundt pan.

Bake at 325 degrees for 1 hour and 10 minutes or until the cake tests done. Cool in the pan for 10 to 15 minutes; remove to a serving plate.

Spread Creamy Chocolate Glaze on the cake.

Creamy Chocolate Glaze

Ingredients

2¼	cups sifted confectioners' sugar
3	tablespoons baking cocoa
¼	cup margarine, softened
3	(to 4) tablespoons milk

Combine the confectioners' sugar and baking cocoa in a mixer bowl; mix well. Add the margarine; beat well. Add enough milk to make of spreading consistency, beating until smooth.

yields sixteen servings

Cream Cheese Pound Cake

Ingredients

1½	cups margarine, softened
8	ounces cream cheese, softened
3	cups sugar
	Dash of salt
1½	teaspoons vanilla extract
6	large eggs
3	cups flour

Bring all ingredients to room temperature. Cream the margarine, cream cheese and sugar in a mixer bowl until light and fluffy. Add the salt and vanilla. Add eggs 1 at a time, beating well after each addition. Add the flour; beat well. Spoon into a greased tube pan. Place cake pan in a cold oven.

Bake at 325 degrees for 1½ hours or until the cake tests done. Cool in the pan for 10 minutes; remove to a wire rack to cool completely.

yields twelve servings

Lavender Pound Cake

Ingredients

1	cup butter, softened
2	cups sugar
5	egg yolks
3	cups flour
½	teaspoon baking soda
	Pinch of salt
1	cup buttermilk
2	teaspoons vanilla extract
5	egg whites, stiffly beaten
½	cup crushed dried lavender petals

A pound cake was originally called a "pound cake" because it was made with a pound of flour, a pound of sugar, a pound of butter and a pound of eggs.

✌ Cream the butter and sugar in a mixer bowl until light and fluffy. Add egg yolks 1 at a time, beating well after each addition. Mix the flour, baking soda and salt together. Add to the creamed mixture alternately with the buttermilk, beating well. Add the vanilla. Fold in the egg whites and lavender. Spoon into a greased and floured 10-inch tube pan.

✌ Bake at 350 degrees for 50 to 60 minutes or until the cake tests done. Cool in the pan for several minutes; remove to a wire rack to cool completely.

✌ Do not substitute margarine for the butter in this recipe.

yields sixteen servings

Apple Sheet Pie

Ingredients

5	cups flour
1	teaspoon salt
2½	cups shortening
1	egg
2	teaspoons vinegar
15	(to 20) medium apples, peeled, sliced
½	cup sugar
3	tablespoons flour
2	tablespoons cinnamon
2	cups confectioners' sugar
2	tablespoons butter, softened
3	ounces cream cheese, softened
2	(to 3) tablespoons milk
1	cup chopped pecans

Combine 5 cups flour and salt in a bowl. Cut in the shortening with a pastry blender until crumbly. Place the egg and vinegar in a measuring cup. Add enough cold water to measure 1 cup; stir to mix. Add to the dry ingredients; mix well. Chill, covered, in refrigerator for 1 hour. Divide the dough into 2 portions, one slightly larger than the other. Roll the larger portion on a floured surface to 2 inches larger than a 13x18-inch baking pan. Place the pastry in a baking pan.

Combine the apples, sugar, 3 tablespoons flour and cinnamon in a large bowl, tossing to mix. Spread over the pastry in the baking pan. Roll the remaining portion of dough to fit over the apples. Place over the apples, crimping edges together with a fork to seal and cutting several vents in the top.

Bake at 425 degrees for 1 hour. Let cool for 2 hours.

Beat the confectioners' sugar, butter and cream cheese in a mixer bowl. Add the milk; beat until creamy. Stir in the pecans. Spread over the cooled pie. Chill until serving time.

yields fifty (one-inch) pieces

Buttermilk Pie

Ingredients

3	eggs, beaten
½	cup melted butter
2	cups sugar
3	tablespoons flour
1	teaspoon vanilla extract
1	cup buttermilk
1	unbaked (10-inch) deep-dish pie shell

Combine the eggs, butter, sugar, flour, vanilla and buttermilk in a mixer bowl; beat well. Pour into the pie shell.

Bake at 350 degrees for 40 to 45 minutes or until the custard is set.

yields eight servings

Peaches-and-Cream Pie

Ingredients

¾	cup sugar
½	cup flour
2	cups sliced fresh peaches
1	unbaked (9-inch) pie shell
1	cup whipping cream

Mix the sugar and flour in a bowl. Arrange half of the peaches in the unbaked pie shell. Sprinkle with half of the sugar mixture. Add the remaining peaches; sprinkle with the remaining sugar mixture. Pour the cream over the peaches, pressing peaches under the cream with a spoon.

Bake at 350 degrees for 40 to 45 minutes. Cool for 1 to 1½ hours or until set.

yields eight servings

A cut-glass pitcher filled with flowers is all that is needed for an elegant table setting.

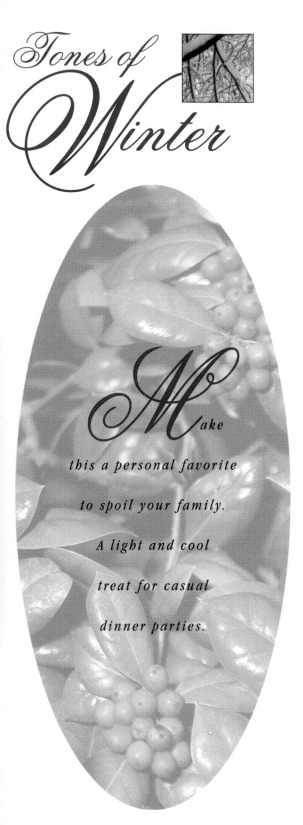

Make

this a personal favorite

to spoil your family.

A light and cool

treat for casual

dinner parties.

Strawberry Chiffon Pie

Ingredients

1¼	cups fine graham cracker crumbs
3	tablespoons sugar
⅓	(to ½) cup butter, softened
1	(3-ounce) package strawberry gelatin
1	cup boiling water
3	egg yolks
1	tablespoon lemon juice
¼	teaspoon salt
¼	cup sugar
1½	cups sliced fresh strawberries
3	egg whites
2	tablespoons sugar
½	cup whipping cream, whipped

Combine the graham cracker crumbs, sugar and butter in a bowl; mix well. Add 1 to 2 tablespoons water or enough to blend the mixture. Press over the bottom and side of a 9-inch pie plate.

Bake at 350 degrees for 10 minutes. Cool.

Dissolve the gelatin in the boiling water in a bowl. Combine the egg yolks, lemon juice, salt and ¼ cup sugar in a double boiler. Cook over hot water until the mixture thickens, whisking constantly. Remove from the heat. Stir in the gelatin.

Place the strawberries in a blender container; process until puréed. Stir into the gelatin mixture. Chill in refrigerator for 1 hour or until partially set.

Beat the egg whites in a mixer bowl until soft peaks form. Add 2 tablespoons sugar gradually, beating until stiff. Fold into the gelatin mixture. Spoon into the graham cracker pie shell. Chill until serving time. Top with the whipped cream and garnish with several whole strawberries.

yields eight servings

Coconut Caramel Pies

Ingredients

7	ounces shredded coconut
1	cup (or more) chopped pecans
¼	cup butter
8	ounces light cream cheese, softened
1	(14-ounce) can sweetened condensed milk
8	ounces whipped topping
1	(12-ounce) jar caramel ice cream topping
2	baked (10-inch) deep-dish pie shells

Brown the coconut and pecans in the butter in a skillet, stirring constantly. Combine the cream cheese and condensed milk in a mixer bowl; beat well. Fold in the whipped topping.

Layer half the cream cheese mixture, half the ice cream topping and half the pecan mixture ¼ at a time in 1 pie shell. Repeat the layers in the remaining pie shell. Freeze, covered, until 5 minutes before serving time. Let stand at room temperature. Slice; top with additional ice cream topping if desired.

yields sixteen servings

Tones of Winter

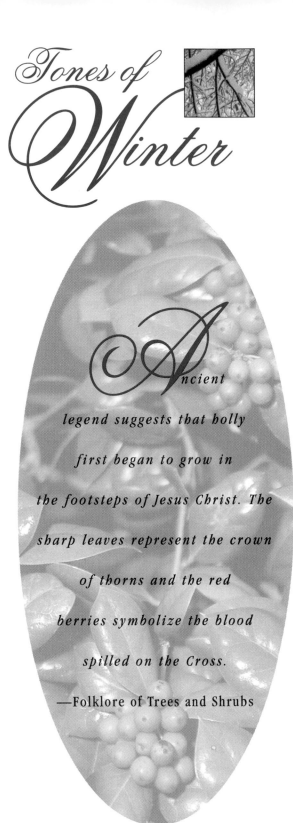

Fresh Fruit Tart

Ingredients

1	cup flour
1	tablespoon sugar
½	teaspoon salt
5	tablespoons shortening, chilled
3	tablespoons unsalted butter, chilled, cut into pieces
3	tablespoons ice water
8	ounces cream cheese, softened
¼	cup sugar
2½	teaspoons fresh lemon juice
½	cup whipping cream, chilled
3	kiwifruit, peeled, sliced
½	cup each strawberry halves, blueberries and orange sections
¼	cup apricot preserves
1	tablespoon water

Mix the flour, 1 tablespoon sugar and salt in a bowl. Cut in the shortening and butter with a pastry blender until crumbly. Add just enough ice water 1 tablespoon at a time to form a dough. Shape into a ball and flatten. Chill, wrapped in plastic wrap, for 30 minutes. Roll out on a lightly floured surface to ⅛-inch thickness; place in a greased 9-inch springform pan. Trim and crimp the edges. Chill for 30 minutes. Cover with foil; fill with dried beans or a pie weight.

Bake at 375 degrees for 15 minutes. Remove the beans and foil. Bake for 10 minutes longer or until golden brown. Cool completely.

Beat the cream cheese, ¼ cup sugar and lemon juice in a mixer bowl until blended. Add the whipping cream, beating until light and fluffy. Spread the filling in the cooled crust. Chill for 8 to 10 hours. Arrange the fruit in concentric circles over the filling. May chill for up to 3 hours.

Combine the preserves and water in a saucepan. Bring to a boil, stirring constantly. Brush the glaze over the fruit just before serving.

yields eight servings

Pear Almond Tart

Ingredients

1½	cups plus 1 tablespoon unbleached flour
½	cup plus 2 tablespoons sugar
	Pinch each of salt and cloves
½	teaspoon grated lemon peel
½	cup cold unsalted butter
1	egg yolk
5	tablespoons ice water
½	cup apricot preserves
2	tablespoons dark rum
½	cup finely ground almonds
7	firm ripe pears, peeled

❧ Process 1½ cups of the flour, 2 tablespoons of the sugar, salt, cloves and lemon peel in a food processor fitted with metal chopping blade until just mixed. Add the butter; process until crumbly. Add the egg yolk; process until blended. Add the ice water; process for several seconds or until the mixture forms a ball. Do not overmix. Chill, wrapped in plastic wrap, for 1 hour or longer. Roll dough out slightly larger than a 10-inch springform pan. Place in a buttered springform pan, pressing gently against the bottom and side. Trim the edges; prick the bottom and side with a fork. Chill for 30 minutes. Cover with foil; fill with dried beans.

❧ Bake at 375 degrees for 15 minutes. Remove dried beans and foil. Bake for 5 minutes longer. Cool completely.

❧ Combine the preserves and rum in a saucepan. Heat over low heat, stirring constantly until well mixed; strain. Brush the tart shell with 2 tablespoons of the glaze. Sprinkle with mixture of almonds, remaining ½ cup sugar and remaining flour. Cut the pears into halves lengthwise; remove cores. Cut pear halves crosswise. Arrange pears in a circle over almond mixture. Chop any remaining pears and fill spaces.

❧ Bake at 375 degrees for 40 minutes. Brush with remaining glaze. Serve at room temperature.

yields eight servings

A particularly sweet version of an old favorite. Dark corn syrup may be substituted for the sorghum molasses.

Tennessee Pecan Pie

Ingredients

2	cups pecan halves
1	unbaked (9-inch) pie shell
3	eggs
⅛	teaspoon salt
½	cup sugar
1	cup sorghum molasses
½	cup melted butter
½	teaspoon vanilla extract

Chop ¼ cup of the pecan halves; spread in the pie shell. Beat the eggs and salt in a mixer bowl until the mixture thickens. Add the sugar gradually, beating well. Stir in the molasses, butter and vanilla; spoon into the pie shell. Spread the remaining 1¾ cups pecan halves on top. Bake at 350 degrees for 1 hour.

yields eight servings

Blackberry Cobbler

Ingredients

3	cups flour
1	teaspoon salt
1	cup shortening
7	(to 9) tablespoons ice water
1	cup sugar
¼	cup flour
2	tablespoons plus 2 teaspoons margarine
1½	quarts blackberries

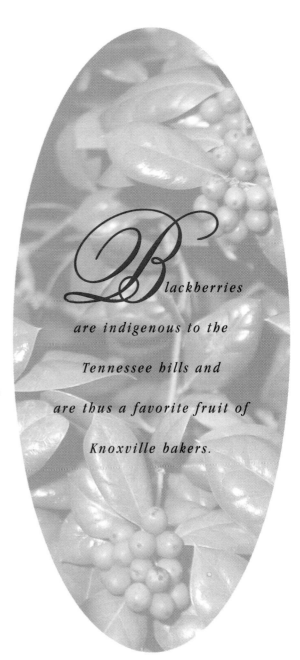

Combine 3 cups flour and salt in a bowl. Cut in the shortening until crumbly. Stir in the ice water 1 tablespoon at a time until the dough forms a ball. Chill, wrapped in plastic wrap, in refrigerator.

Combine the sugar and ¼ cup flour in a bowl. Cut in the margarine until crumbly. Combine with the blackberries in a saucepan. Simmer for several minutes, stirring constantly until well mixed.

Divide the dough into 2 portions, 1 larger than the other. Roll out larger portion of dough on a floured surface to fit a 1½ quart baking dish. Fit the dough into a buttered baking dish. Spoon in the blackberry mixture. Roll the remaining dough on a floured surface; place over the berries. Crimp the edges together and pierce the top with a fork. Sprinkle with a small amount of additional sugar.

Bake at 375 degrees for 30 to 40 minutes or until golden brown. Serve with ice cream.

yields eight servings

Blackberries are indigenous to the Tennessee hills and are thus a favorite fruit of Knoxville bakers.

Tones of Winter

"Out-of-This-League" Brownies

Ingredients

½	cup butter, softened
½	cup peanut butter
½	cup packed brown sugar
½	cup sugar
2	eggs
2	teaspoons vanilla extract
½	cup flour
1	cup quick-cooking oats
¼	cup baking cocoa
1	teaspoon baking soda
¾	cup semisweet chocolate chips
½	cup milk chocolate chips
½	cup white chocolate chips
1	cup chopped pecans

Combine the butter, peanut butter, brown sugar and sugar in a mixer bowl; beat until creamy. Add the eggs and vanilla; beat well.

Mix the flour, oats, baking cocoa and baking soda in a bowl. Stir into the egg mixture until blended. Add the chocolate chips and pecans; mix well. Spoon into a greased 9x13-inch baking dish.

Bake at 350 degrees for 18 to 22 minutes or until the edges pull from the sides of the baking dish. Do not overbake. Cool completely before cutting.

yields fifteen servings

Date-Nut Bars

Ingredients

½	cup butter, softened
½	cup sugar
½	cup flour
½	teaspoon baking powder
¼	teaspoon salt
1	egg, beaten
1	cup chopped dates
¼	cup chopped walnuts or pecans
¼	cup sifted confectioners' sugar

Cream the butter and sugar in a mixer bowl until light and fluffy. Sift the flour, baking powder and salt together. Add to the creamed mixture; mix well. Add the egg; beat well. Stir in the dates and walnuts. Spoon into a greased 9x13 inch baking dish.

Bake at 325 degrees for 30 minutes. Cool and cut into 1-inch bars. Sprinkle confectioners' sugar over the top.

yields fifteen servings

Fill a small bean basket with items for your bridge-playing friend: Include pretty recipe cards for Ginger Tea, Holiday Shortbread and Date Nut Bars, a set of playing cards, some colorful cocktail napkins and a batch of the Date-Nut Bars.

Tones of Winter

Ginger Cookies

Ingredients

⅔	cup shortening
1	cup sugar
1	egg, beaten
2	tablespoons molasses
2	tablespoons dark corn syrup
2	cups flour
2	teaspoons baking soda
½	teaspoon cloves
½	teaspoon cinnamon
½	teaspoon ginger
½	teaspoon salt
½	cup (or more) sugar

Cream the shortening and 1 cup sugar in a mixer bowl until light and fluffy. Add the egg, molasses and corn syrup; mix well. Sift the flour, baking soda, cloves, cinnamon, ginger and salt together. Add to the creamed mixture; mix well. Batter will be very stiff. Roll into balls by teaspoonfuls; coat with the remaining sugar. Place on a nonstick cookie sheet.

Bake at 350 degrees for 12 to 15 minutes or until brown. Cookies will crack as they bake and be crisp on the outside with a chewy middle. Cool on cookie sheet for several minutes; remove to wire rack to cool completely. May use tinted sugar to coat cookies before baking.

yields forty cookies

Lemon Sugar Cookies

Ingredients

4	large eggs
1½	cups vegetable oil
4	cups flour
4	teaspoons baking powder
1½	cups sugar
4	teaspoons (heaping) grated lemon peel
4	teaspoons vanilla extract
	Frosting

Combine the eggs and oil in a mixer bowl; beat at medium speed until well blended. Mix the flour, baking powder and sugar together. Add to the egg mixture; beat well. Stir in the lemon peel and vanilla. Drop by heaping teaspoonfuls onto a nonstick cookie sheet.

Bake at 350 degrees for 10 to 12 minutes. Cool on cookie sheet for several minutes; remove to a wire rack to cool completely. Spread Frosting on cooled cookies.

Frosting

Ingredients

2½	cups confectioners' sugar
1	tablespoon melted margarine
2	tablespoons lemon juice
1	tablespoon water
½	teaspoon vanilla extract

Combine the confectioners' sugar, margarine, lemon juice, water and vanilla in a mixer bowl; beat well.

yields forty-eight cookies

Decorate a basket with holiday colors; fill with a selection of cookies for a child's dream come true!

Holiday Shortbread

Ingredients

1	cup butter, softened
1	cup sugar
2¼	cups flour
1	egg yolk
1	teaspoon vanilla extract
1	egg white, lightly beaten
½	cup chopped almonds
¼	cup red and/or green tinted sugar

Cream the butter and sugar in a mixer bowl until light and fluffy. Add the flour; mix well. Add the egg yolk and vanilla; mix well. Spread the mixture in a greased 9x13-inch baking dish. Spread the egg white over the top; sprinkle with the almonds and tinted sugar.

Bake at 350 degrees for 25 minutes. Cool before cutting into squares.

yields fifteen servings

Chocolate Almond Biscotti

Ingredients

½	cup butter, softened
1¼	cups sugar
2	eggs
1	teaspoon almond extract
2¼	cups flour
¼	cup premium European-style cocoa
1	teaspoon baking powder
¼	teaspoon salt
1	cup sliced almonds
1	cup semisweet chocolate chips
1	tablespoon plus 1 teaspoon shortening
¼	cup each vanilla milk chips and sliced almonds

Cream the butter and sugar in a mixer bowl until light and fluffy. Add the eggs and almond extract; mix well. Add mixture of the flour, cocoa, baking powder and salt; mix well. Stir in 1 cup almonds. Divide dough into 2 portions. Shape each into an 11-inch log; place the logs 2 inches apart on a nonstick cookie sheet.

Bake at 375 degrees on the middle oven rack for 30 minutes or until firm. Cool on the cookie sheet for 15 minutes. Cut the logs diagonally with a serrated knife into ½-inch slices, discarding the end pieces. Arrange the slices cut side down close together on 2 nonstick cookie sheets. Bake at 375 degrees for 26 minutes, turning cookies after 13 minutes. Cool on cookie sheets.

Combine the chocolate chips and 1 tablespoon of the shortening in a glass bowl. Microwave on High for 1 to 1½ minutes or until melted; stir until smooth. Dip ends of the biscotti into the chocolate glaze or drizzle the glaze over the biscotti.

Combine the vanilla chips and remaining 1 teaspoon shortening in a glass bowl. Microwave on High for 30 to 45 seconds or until melted; stir until smooth. Drizzle over the glaze. Top with sliced almonds. Store in an airtight container.

yields twenty-eight cookies

Listen! A

melting icicle's metronome

drip breaks winter

silence along the black

slate brows of

Alum Cave Bluffs on

one of the park's most

popular trails.

—Wilma Dykeman
Explorations

Napkins, Knives & Knoxville

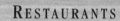

RESTAURANTS

CELEBRITIES

*M*any

(Tennesseans) were farmers

who hated wars and suspected any

standing army, but they did

not shun a fight. Indeed, their vivid

nickname—the Volunteers—

reflects the readiness with

which ordinary citizens rallied

to the call to arms: . . .

—*Wilma Dykeman*
Tennessee,
A History

Restaurants

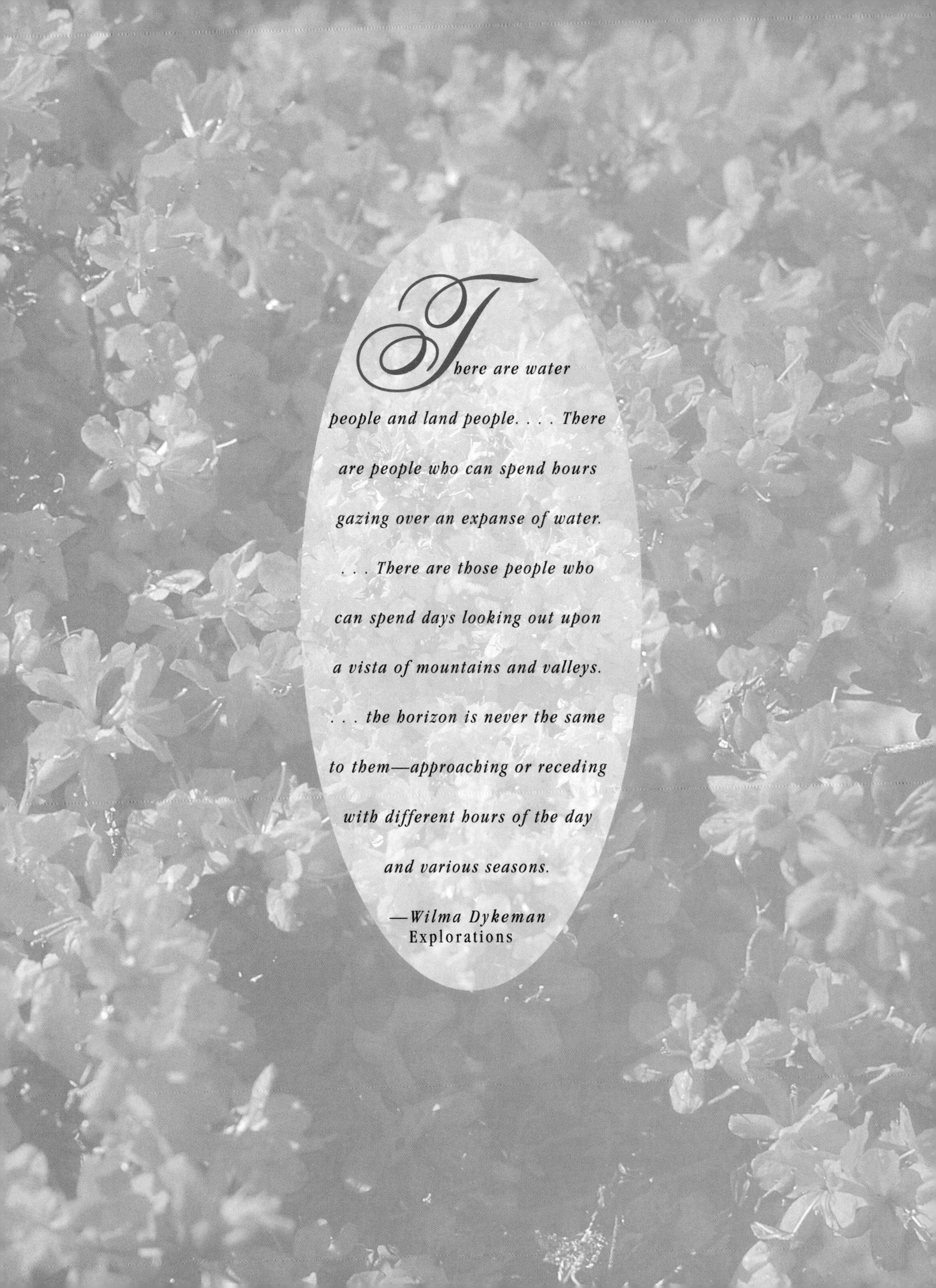

There are water people and land people. . . . There are people who can spend hours gazing over an expanse of water. . . . There are those people who can spend days looking out upon a vista of mountains and valleys. . . . the horizon is never the same to them—approaching or receding with different hours of the day and various seasons.

—*Wilma Dykeman*
Explorations

Arizona Spuds

Ingredients

5	fresh potatoes or leftover baked potatoes
1	onion
1	cup sour cream
½	cup milk
1	(10-ounce) can cream of mushroom soup
	Salt and pepper to taste
1	cup shredded cheese
2	cups crushed cornflakes
2	tablespoons melted margarine

Slice the potatoes and onion; place in a bowl. Add the sour cream, milk, soup, salt and pepper; toss to mix. Spoon the mixture into a greased 9x13-inch baking dish. Sprinkle the cheese and a mixture of the cornflakes and margarine over the top.

Bake at 350 degrees for 1 hour.

yields ten servings

*R*enowned

for the "Best Burger in

Knoxville," this former meat

market has been frequented

for years by Fountain City

residents who have enjoyed

its relaxed atmosphere

and kitschy decor.

Litton's Market and Restaurant

Caramel Fudge Cake

Ingredients

3	(5-ounce) Hershey's plain chocolate bars
1	(8-ounce) can Hershey's syrup
½	cup margarine, softened
2	cups sugar
4	eggs
1½	cups buttermilk
1	teaspoon baking soda
4	cups flour, sifted
1	tablespoon vanilla extract
	Ice cream
	Caramel sauce, heated

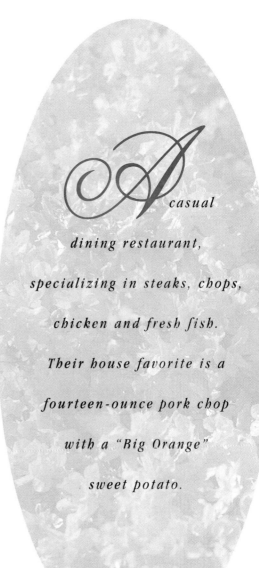

Combine the Hershey bars and syrup in a double boiler. Melt over hot water, stirring until mixed.

Cream the margarine and sugar in a mixer bowl until light and fluffy. Add the eggs 1 at a time, beating well after each addition. Add the chocolate mixture; mix well.

Combine the buttermilk, baking soda and vanilla in a bowl; beat until foamy. Add the buttermilk mixture alternately with the flour to the creamed mixture, beating just until mixed.

Spray a 9x13-inch baking dish with nonstick baking spray. Line with waxed paper; spray with nonstick baking spray. Spoon the batter into the prepared dish.

Bake at 350 degrees for 1 hour or until the cake tests done.

Serve with ice cream; drizzle with hot caramel sauce.

yields fifteen servings

A casual dining restaurant, specializing in steaks, chops, chicken and fresh fish. Their house favorite is a fourteen-ounce pork chop with a "Big Orange" sweet potato.

The Chop House

Red Velvet Cake

Ingredients

3⅓	cups flour
¼	teaspoon salt
¾	teaspoon baking soda
¾	teaspoon baking powder
¾	cup butter, softened
2⅔	cups sugar
5	eggs
1⅓	cups buttermilk
2	tablespoons plus 1 teaspoon red food coloring
	Red Velvet Icing
2	tablespoons flaked coconut
	Several drops of red food coloring

❧ Sift the flour, salt, baking soda and baking powder together. Cream the butter and sugar in a mixer bowl until light and fluffy. Add the eggs 1 at a time, beating well after each addition. Add the flour mixture gradually, beating at medium speed and scraping the sides of the bowl occasionally. Add the buttermilk and 2 tablespoons plus 1 teaspoon food coloring gradually; beat for 2 minutes. Spoon the batter into 3 greased and floured 9-inch cake pans.

❧ Bake at 350 degrees for 25 to 30 minutes or until the cake tests done. Cool in the pans for several minutes; remove to a wire rack to cool for 15 minutes.

❧ Spread the icing between layers and over the top and side of the cake.

❧ Moisten the coconut with several drops of red food coloring, stirring to mix. Sprinkle the coconut over the top of cake.

Red Velvet Icing

Ingredients

½	cup butter, softened
4	cups confectioners' sugar
½	cup whipping cream
1	tablespoon vanilla extract

❧ Cream the butter and confectioners' sugar in a mixer bowl until light and fluffy. Add the cream gradually, beating well. Add the vanilla.

A Knoxville tradition since 1919 and founded by the Regas brothers as an eighteen-stool coffee shop, this successful restaurant with its varied American menu is host to business luncheons and festive dinners alike.

Regas

yields twelve servings

A Spring Fool

Ingredients

1	cup chopped rhubarb
½	cup sugar
½	cup water
1½	cups strawberry halves
1	cup whipping cream
1	tablespoon brown sugar
	Sesame Lace Cookie Bowls

Combine the rhubarb, sugar and water in a saucepan. Simmer over medium heat until the rhubarb is tender, stirring occasionally. Cook over high heat until the water is evaporated and the mixture is the consistency of syrup, stirring frequently. Add the strawberries. Remove from the heat. Cover and let stand for 15 minutes. Process in a food processor until the strawberries are puréed. Let cool.

Whip the cream in a mixer bowl until soft peaks form. Add the brown sugar gradually, beating until stiff. Fold into the puréed mixture. Spoon into Sesame Lace Cookie Bowls. Garnish with fresh berries.

Sesame Lace Cookie Bowls

Ingredients

10	tablespoons butter
½	cup plus 2 tablespoons light corn syrup
8	ounces brown sugar
2	tablespoons sesame oil
1½	cups flour
¼	cup sesame seeds
2	tablespoons black sesame seeds, optional

Combine the butter, corn syrup, brown sugar and sesame oil in a saucepan. Bring to a boil, stirring constantly. Remove from the heat; stir in the flour and sesame seeds. Pour into a large shallow pan and let cool. Scoop the mixture with an ice cream scoop and drop 2 inches apart on a nonstick cookie sheet.

Bake at 350 degrees for 9 minutes. Cool for 2 minutes. Lift the cookies with a spatula; place on inverted soup bowls, shaping gently around bowl. Cool completely. Lift the cookie bowls carefully; place on a serving dish.

yields twenty-five servings

*W*hether staying for a romantic getaway weekend or honing up on your fly-fishing, you will find that this five-star inn nestled in the Smokies, with its gourmet cuisine and luxurious appointments, will awaken all of your senses.

The Inn At Blackberry Farm

Napkins, Knives & Knoxville

Spaghetti Carbonara

Ingredients

1	cup sliced mushrooms
1	cup green peas
1	cup finely chopped onion
1	cup prosciutto ham slivers
1	tablespoon milled black pepper
½	teaspoon salt
¼	cup olive oil
1	cup grated Parmesan cheese
4	eggs
¼	cup chopped fresh parsley
16	ounces spaghetti, cooked

Sauté the mushrooms, peas, onion and ham with the pepper and salt in the olive oil in a large skillet. Stir in the cheese, eggs and parsley; mix well. Cook until the eggs are set, stirring frequently. Add the cooked spaghetti; toss to mix.

yields six servings

*A*uthentic

Italian cuisine and

a warm, cozy atmosphere

bring Knoxvillians back

on a regular basis for

a relaxing evening out.

Naples Italian Restaurant

Sweet Potato Casserole

Ingredients

2½	pounds sweet potatoes
¼	cup margarine, softened
½	cup sugar
1	cup half-and-half
3	eggs
¼	cup margarine
½	cup packed brown sugar
1	cup cornflakes, coarsely crumbled
⅓	cup chopped pecans
⅓	cup chopped walnuts
2	cups miniature marshmallows

Combine the sweet potatoes and enough water to cover in a saucepan. Boil until the sweet potatoes are tender; drain and cool. Remove the peelings.

Mash the sweet potatoes in a bowl. Add ¼ cup margarine, sugar, half-and-half and eggs; mix well. Spread in a greased 7x11-inch baking pan sprayed with nonstick baking spray.

Melt the remaining ¼ cup margarine in a saucepan over medium heat. Add the brown sugar; cook until melted, stirring until well mixed. Remove from the heat. Stir in the cornflake crumbs, pecans, walnuts and marshmallows. Spread the topping over the sweet potatoes.

Bake at 375 degrees for 20 to 30 minutes or until heated through.

yields six servings

A nineties' approach to a fifties' fad! Great American cuisine featuring daily "Blue Plate" specials and tempting desserts in a casual, open setting.

The Diner

Polynesian Chicken Salad

Ingredients

2	pounds boneless chicken breasts
2½	cups sliced celery
1	(16-ounce) can pineapple chunks, drained
1¼	cups red seedless grape halves
¾	cup shredded carrot
1	cup mayonnaise
½	cup sour cream
2	teaspoons each curry powder and lemon juice
1	teaspoon salt

Rinse the chicken. Simmer the chicken in enough salted water to cover in a saucepan for 25 minutes or just until cooked through; drain. Cool and chop the chicken.

Combine the celery, pineapple, grapes, carrot and chicken in a bowl; mix well. Add mixture of remaining ingredients; toss to mix.

yields eight cups

Whether at the downtown or the west Knoxville location, this is where Knoxvillians gather regularly for varied and delicious luncheon fare in a casual, friendly atmosphere.

The Lunchbox

Grasshopper Pie

Ingredients

2	cups milk
2	(4-ounce) packages vanilla instant pudding mix
1	teaspoon peppermint extract
1	teaspoon chocolate-flavor extract
1	teaspoon green food coloring
6	ounces whipped topping
1	(9-inch) chocolate crumb pie shell
6	tablespoons (heaping) whipped topping
6	tablespoons chocolate syrup

Combine the milk, pudding mix, flavorings and food coloring in a bowl; beat until thickened. Stir in 6 ounces whipped topping. Spoon into a chocolate pie shell. Freeze until set.

Serve frozen or partially thawed with a dollop of whipped topping on top. Drizzle with chocolate syrup.

yields six servings

Families continue to enjoy the novelty of catching their own fish for dinner and "diving" into sumptuous homemade desserts at this country hideaway outside of Knoxville.

The Crosseyed Cricket

Apple Fritters

Ingredients

½	cup milk
1	egg
2	tablespoons melted butter
1	teaspoon vanilla extract
1½	cups cake flour
¼	teaspoon salt
1	tablespoon baking powder
½	cup sugar
1	tablespoon grated orange peel
½	cup chopped unpeeled apple
	Vegetable oil for deep-frying

Combine the milk, egg, butter and vanilla in a bowl; mix well. Add a mixture of flour, salt, baking powder and sugar; mix well. Stir in the orange peel and apple.

Drop by spoonfuls into 325-degree oil in deep fryer and fry until golden brown; drain.

yields twelve servings

Once guests have savored the special taste of hot apple fritters, they return often to this charmingly rustic restaurant in the Smokies.

Applewood Restaurant

216

Chili

Ingredients

2	pounds ground beef
1	large yellow onion, finely chopped
1	(32-ounce) can pinto beans
1	(32-ounce) can red chili beans
1	(32-ounce) can tomato sauce
1	teaspoon salt
2	teaspoons granulated garlic
1	teaspoon ground pepper
¼	cup chili powder
1	(4 ounce) can chili con carne
4	cups beef stock

Brown the ground beef with the onion in a skillet, stirring until the ground beef is crumbly; drain. Combine the pinto beans, red chili beans, tomato sauce, salt, garlic, pepper, chili powder and chili con carne in a large stockpot; mix well. Add the cooked ground beef mixture and beef stock. Simmer for 30 minutes, stirring occasionally.

yields twenty servings

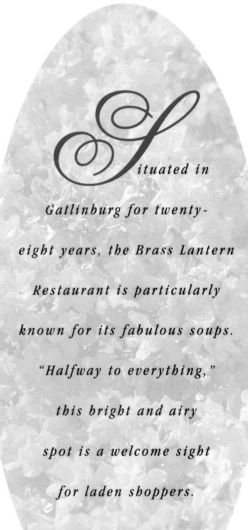

Situated in Gatlinburg for twenty-eight years, the Brass Lantern Restaurant is particularly known for its fabulous soups. "Halfway to everything," this bright and airy spot is a welcome sight for laden shoppers.

Brass Lantern Restaurant

Black Bean Soup

Ingredients

4	cups black beans
1½	gallons water
1	ham hock with ham
1	cup finely chopped red onion
½	tablespoon ground pepper
½	tablespoon salt
1	tablespoon cumin
1	tablespoon garlic in oil
1	tablespoon Tabasco sauce

Combine the black beans and 1 gallon of the water in a large stockpot. Trim ham from ham hock; chop into slivers. Add ham and ham hock to the stockpot. Add the onion, pepper, salt, cumin, garlic and Tabasco sauce; mix well.

Cook over high heat for 2 hours, stirring frequently. Add the remaining ½ gallon water. Cook until the beans are soft. Remove the ham hock; stir beans with a wire whisk.

yields sixteen cups

*L*ocated in the heart of Gatlinburg and famous for their hearty, country cuisine (especially breakfast!), this establishment provides the perfect landing for weary hikers.

Burning Bush Restaurant

Bran Muffins

Ingredients

1	cup boiling water
3	cups All-Bran cereal
1	cup margarine, softened
1½	cups sugar
2	eggs
2½	cups flour
2½	teaspoons baking soda
1	teaspoon salt
2	cups buttermilk

Pour the water over the cereal in a bowl. Let stand until softened. Cream the margarine and sugar in a mixer bowl until light and fluffy. Beat the eggs 1 at a time. Sift the dry ingredients together. Add to the creamed mixture alternately with the buttermilk; mix well. Stir in the cereal. Fill greased muffin cups ¾ full.

Bake at 400 degrees for 15 minutes or until the muffins test done.

yields forty servings

Customers are greeted with a basket of these mini muffins, hot out of the oven and served with the tea room's special honey-butter, upon their arrival to this traditional log cabin.

Apple Cake Tea Room

Baked Mushrooms Stuffed with Crab Imperial

Gleaming copper tables, rich dark wood and supple leather seats make for an inviting atmosphere for a rendezvous with that special someone or after a hard day at the office.

Copper Cellar

Ingredients

1½	tablespoons chopped parsley
⅛	teaspoon cayenne
1	teaspoon dry mustard
¼	teaspoon baking powder
¼	teaspoon Worcestershire sauce
½	tablespoon lemon juice
¾	cup mayonnaise
1	egg, beaten
1	pound Blue Crab meat, shell removed
45	large mushrooms
1	cup fresh bread crumbs

Combine the parsley, cayenne, mustard, baking powder, Worcestershire sauce, lemon juice, mayonnaise and egg in a bowl; mix well. Add the crab meat, mixing gently.

Rinse the mushrooms; pat dry. Remove the stems. Fill each mushroom cap with about 1 tablespoonful of the crab meat mixture; sprinkle with the bread crumbs. Arrange stuffed mushrooms so they do not touch in 2 greased 9x13-inch baking dishes.

Bake at 350 degrees for 15 to 18 minutes or until light brown.

yields fifteen servings

Cole Slaw

Ingredients

- ¼ cup sugar
- ¼ cup white vinegar
- 1 teaspoon celery seeds
- 2 cups mayonnaise
- 2¼ pounds green cabbage, shredded
- ½ cup chopped green onions
- ½ cup shredded carrot

Combine the sugar, vinegar and celery seeds in a bowl; mix until the sugar is dissolved. Add the mayonnaise; mix well. Add the cabbage and green onions, tossing lightly to mix. Add the carrot just before serving; mix well.

yields ten servings

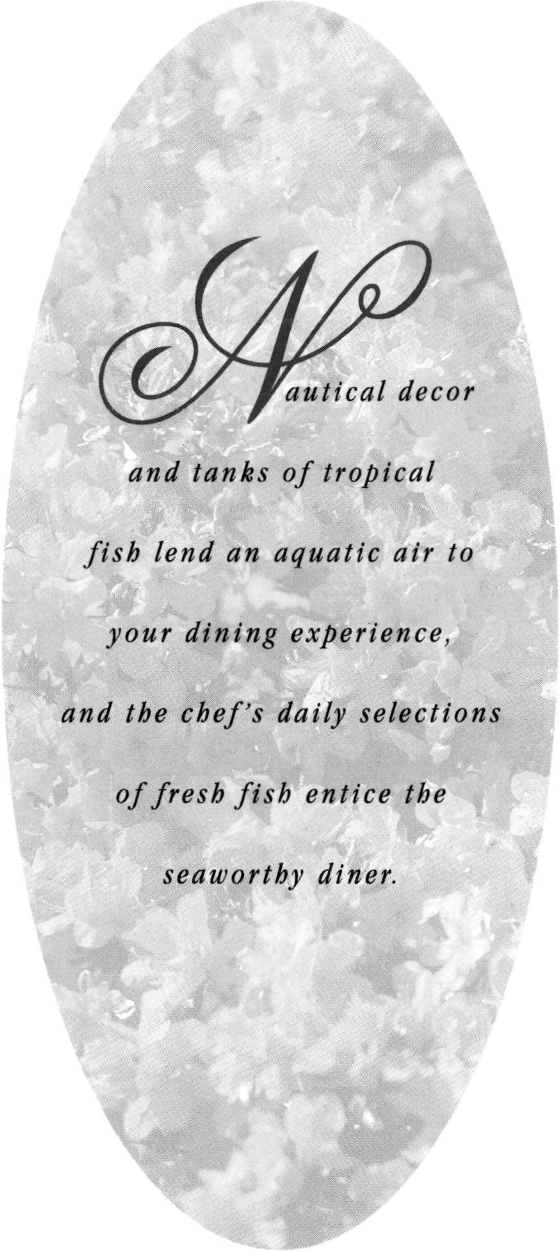

Chesapeake's

Spinach Maria

Their numerous locations are favorite meeting places for UT sports fans. Winner of the "Best Ribs in America" contest for 1988.

Calhoun's

Ingredients

4½	cups milk
1	teaspoon dry mustard
1	teaspoon granulated garlic
½	tablespoon crushed red pepper
1½	pounds Velveeta cheese
½	medium yellow onion
1	tablespoon butter
5	tablespoons melted butter
6	tablespoons flour
5	(10-ounce) packages frozen chopped spinach, thawed
1	cup shredded Monterey Jack cheese

Heat the milk with the mustard, garlic and red pepper in a saucepan to 190 degrees, just below the boiling point, stirring frequently. Reduce the heat.

Crumble the Velveeta cheese into a glass bowl. Microwave until melted. Add to the milk mixture, stirring until mixed.

Sauté the onion in 1 tablespoon butter in a skillet. Add to the cheese sauce.

Combine 5 tablespoons melted butter and flour in a small skillet; mix until blended. Cook over low heat for 3 to 4 minutes to make a roux, stirring constantly. Add the roux to the cheese sauce. Cook over medium heat until the cheese sauce thickens, stirring constantly. Remove from the heat. Cool for 15 minutes.

Squeeze excess water from the thawed spinach. Add to the cheese sauce; mix just until blended. Spoon into 2 greased 9x10-inch baking dishes. Sprinkle each with Monterey Jack cheese.

Bake at 350 degrees for 12 to 15 minutes or until brown.

yields twelve servings

White Chocolate Cheesecake

Ingredients

3	tablespoons unsalted butter, softened
1	cup finely chopped walnuts
24	ounces fine-quality white chocolate, chopped
¾	cup whipping cream, scalded
24	ounces cream cheese, softened
1	cup sugar
¼	cup flour
4	large eggs, at room temperature
1	tablespoon vanilla extract

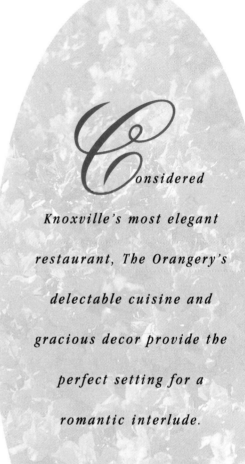

Considered Knoxville's most elegant restaurant, The Orangery's delectable cuisine and gracious decor provide the perfect setting for a romantic interlude.

The Orangery

❧ Coat the bottom and side of a 10-inch springform pan with the butter. Press the walnuts into the butter until coated. Chill in the pan in the freezer for 15 minutes.

❧ Place the white chocolate in a double boiler. Heat over barely simmering water until the chocolate is partially melted, stirring frequently. Add the cream; whisk to mix. Heat until the mixture is smooth, whisking constantly. Remove from the heat.

❧ Combine the cream cheese and sugar in a mixer bowl; mix well. Add the flour and chocolate mixture; mix well. Add the eggs 1 at a time, beating well after each addition. Add the vanilla. Spoon the mixture into the prepared pan.

❧ Bake at 425 degrees on the middle rack of the oven for 20 minutes. Reduce the oven temperature to 300 degrees. Bake for 45 to 55 minutes longer or until the cheesecake is firm in the center and a tester comes out clean. Turn off the oven. Let the cheesecake stand in the oven for 30 minutes. Remove to a wire rack to cool completely. Chill the cheesecake, covered, for at least 6 hours and for up to 24 hours. Run a thin knife around the edge of the pan; remove the side of pan. Cut the cheesecake with a knife dipped in hot water.

yields eight servings

Celebrities

Chili

Chocolate Soda Punch

Mother's Soup

Martha O'Neill's Westport Room Salad

Vegetable Parmesan Pasta Salad

Opossum and Sweet Potatoes

Fresh Tomatoes, Basil and Croutons
with Thin Spaghetti

Stay-At-Home-Tuesday Night Pasta

Fried Green Tomatoes

Our Friend's Chocolate-Mint Dessert

Carrot Cake with Cream Cheese Icing

Dirt Cake

Mrs. Ruth's Famous Chocolate Pie

Pecan Pie

Baked Onions

Corn Bread

Perhaps

one way to define

personality—our own or

another person's —is

to discover the season we

carry within us.

—*Wilma Dykeman*
Explorations

Chili

2	pounds ground beef
1	large onion, chopped
2	tablespoons chili powder
2	tablespoons paprika
2	tablespoons baking cocoa
1	teaspoon salt
½	teaspoon pepper
1	(46-ounce) can tomato juice
2	(16-ounce) cans kidney beans

Brown the ground beef in a saucepan, stirring until crumbly.

Add the onion. Cook until the onion is partially cooked.

Add the chili powder, paprika, baking cocoa, salt and pepper. Stir in the tomato juice. Simmer for 45 minutes.

Stir in the beans. Simmer for 45 minutes longer.

yields eight servings

A pure and captivating soprano, her unforgettable arias and theatric bearing combined with a kind and giving spirit make her a Knoxville treasure.

Mary Costa

Mary Costa has been acclaimed as one of the most radiant sopranos of all time and has appeared on the stage of every leading opera house in the world. She has sung with such greats as Placido Domingo and Luciano Pavarotti. Mary performed in forty-six operas in a career that spanned thirty-one years. Her Metropolitan Opera Company debut was in 1964, and in 1970 she embarked on her first Russian tour at the Bolshoi Opera. She has received numerous honors, including an honorary doctorate of music from Hardin-Simmons University in Texas and the "Women of Distinction" award given by Birmingham-Southern College. In addition to her operatic career, she has also performed for radio, television, films, and recordings. She was the voice for Walt Disney's "Sleeping Beauty." Originally released in 1959, "Sleeping Beauty" is due to be rereleased in 1996.

Mary was born in Knoxville and was a student at Knoxville High when her father retired and moved the family to California. Mary returned to her native city to live in the Spring of 1994. "There's something about the peace and strength of the mountains, the goodness and energy of the people here that is irresistible," says Costa.

Chocolate Soda Punch

This drink was a childhood favorite of Mary Costa's mother, Mrs. John T. Costa, who served it on many occasions, including a special DAR gathering at their lovely home in Los Angeles. This particular recipe was given to Mary by a dear family friend, who grew up in Hazel Costa's kitchen, and it was a tremendous hit served in a silver punch bowl at Mrs. Costa's 100th birthday celebration in Palm Beach, Florida in 1993.

1   cup Hershey's chocolate syrup
6   cups milk
½   gallon vanilla ice cream
1   quart ginger ale, chilled

Combine the chocolate syrup and milk in a punch bowl, stirring to mix. Add half of the ice cream, stirring until melted.

Chill the mixture until serving time.

Place small scoops of remaining ice cream in the punch bowl. Pour in the ginger ale and stir gently.

yields twenty servings

Mary Costa

Napkins, Knives & Knoxville

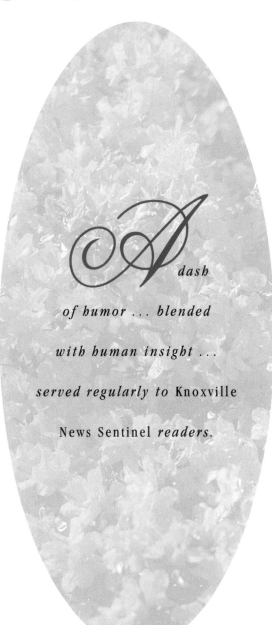

A dash of humor ... blended with human insight ... served regularly to Knoxville News Sentinel readers.

Ina Hughs

Mother's Soup

My mother was a terrible cook, but she made up this recipe and we all loved it!

2	(14-ounce) cans beef broth
2	(14-ounce) cans chicken broth
1	(10-ounce) can tomato soup
	Worcestershire sauce to taste
	Tabasco sauce to taste
	Red pepper to taste
	Sherry to taste

Combine the broths and the tomato soup in a saucepan, stirring until well mixed. Stir in the Worcestershire sauce, Tabasco sauce, red pepper and sherry.

Cook over medium heat until heated through.

yields ten servings

Ina Hughs has been a newspaper columnist for more than twenty years and has been with the *Knoxville News Sentinel* since 1989. Her columns combine a mixture of human insight and humor. Her poem, "A Prayer for Children," is the introduction to her book of the same name. Ina has twice given a reading of this poem on the television program "Good Morning America." The poem has been reprinted in an Ann Landers column and was also read during UNICEF's World Summit for Children.

228

Martha O'Neill's Westport Room Salad

We were given this recipe by friends in Milwaukee. It is very easy and very good. We've even had kids who liked this one.

Dressing:

1	clove of garlic, crushed
1	cup mayonnaise
2	tablespoons grated Parmesan or Romano cheese
1	teaspoon fresh lemon juice
	Salt and pepper to taste
	MSG to taste

Salad:

1	cup herb-seasoned stuffing mix
½	cup butter or margarine
1	head romaine lettuce, torn
½	head iceberg lettuce, torn
½	cup grated fresh cauliflower

Combine the garlic, mayonnaise, cheese, lemon juice, salt, pepper and MSG in a medium bowl. Stir until well mixed, using a small amount of milk to thin the mixture if it is too thick.

Chill, covered, in the refrigerator for 8 to 10 hours.

Sauté the stuffing mix in the butter in a small skillet; set aside.

Toss the lettuce with the chilled dressing in a large salad bowl.

Add the stuffing mix and cauliflower and mix well.

yields eight servings

Sound of pounding

feet on hardwood ...

bright lights ...

cheerleaders yell ...

Swish ... Slam Dunk ...

roar of the crowd ...

hopes for a winning season.

Kevin O'Neill joined the University of Tennessee Athletic Staff in 1994 as the fourteenth head coach for the Vols' basketball team. He came to Knoxville after serving at Marquette University for five years. At age thirty-seven, Kevin is the youngest head coach in the SEC. Martha, his wife, is an avid equestrian.

Kevin and Martha O'Neill

Vegetable Parmesan Pasta Salad

This is a great, easy, simple and delicious pasta salad that is very versatile. The secret is the wonderful dressing. You can use whatever blend of frozen vegetables you like. This recipe can go from side dish to main dish with the addition of 6 chopped cooked chicken breasts.

1	envelope ranch dressing mix
1	cup mayonnaise
1	cup milk or buttermilk
1½	teaspoons cracked black pepper
¾	cup grated Parmesan cheese
1	(16-ounce) package frozen mixed vegetables
1	(16-ounce) package rotini
4.	quarts boiling water
1	tablespoon vegetable oil
1	teaspoon salt
¾	cup canned garbanzo beans (chick-peas), rinsed, drained
¾	cup canned red kidney beans, rinsed, drained

Combine the dressing mix, mayonnaise and milk in a small bowl. Whisk until smooth. Add the pepper and cheese, whisking to mix. Chill while preparing the salad.

Thaw the frozen vegetables, immersing in warm water to cover in a bowl; drain well.

Cook the pasta in 4 quarts boiling water with the oil and salt. Drain and rinse with cold water to cool. Combine the pasta, vegetables, garbanzo beans and kidney beans in a large bowl. Toss well to mix.

Pour the chilled dressing over the pasta mixture, tossing to coat. Chill until serving time.

yields eight servings

*C*ulinary creativity ...

individual style ... highly

demanded talent ... first

choice for Knoxville's fêtes.

David Duncan

David Duncan is a professional caterer, television chef, and gourmet cook. He is a native Knoxvillian and graduated from the University of Tennessee's College of Business. His flair for combining entertainment and creativity is evident on his television show, "Cooking with David Duncan," shown on WATE-TV. Cooking has been a lifelong passion for David since, at the age of five, he asked his mother to help him make his own recipe for chocolate cake. His hobby became his profession after his graduation from UT.

Opossum and Sweet Potatoes

"You can't get away from your raisin'," Joan Wolfe says. A surprising number of folks in this region have tasted this mountain/country delicacy. Joan, a teacher who grew up in a family of nine girls, gave me this recipe, which is a standard. "God invented the opossum so that we'd always have something to eat," I've been told.

1   medium opossum
4   sweet potatoes, cut into halves
     Salt to taste

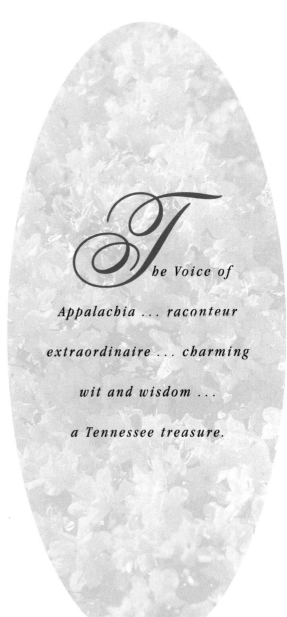

Catch the opossum and clean it out by feeding it molasses, prepared baby food, and honey for a week to ten days.

Kill the opossum and clean it like a chicken. Cut it into serving pieces. Rinse the meat in salted water, changing the water 5 or 6 times.

Place the meat in a pressure cooker, covering with water.

Cook under pressure for 30 minutes. Cool to reduce pressure and remove pieces to a baking dish.

Arrange the sweet potatoes around the meat; sprinkle with salt.

Bake at 350 degrees for 30 minutes.

Serve with cornbread, beans and corn.

yields three servings

The Voice of Appalachia ... raconteur extraordinaire ... charming wit and wisdom ... a Tennessee treasure.

Raconteur extraordinaire Bill Landry is known as the voice of Appalachia. He has been the host/narrator and co-producer of the "Heartland Series" since its beginning in 1984 to commemorate the fiftieth anniversary of the founding of the Great Smoky Mountains National Park. More than 600 five-minute segments have been produced to celebrate the people and the land of the Appalachian region. As well as writing and directing many episodes, Bill has also portrayed various characters for the show. The Heartland Series has won three Emmy Awards, five Iris Awards, and was selected by the United States government to represent the Appalachian culture in all the American embassies around the world.

Bill Landry

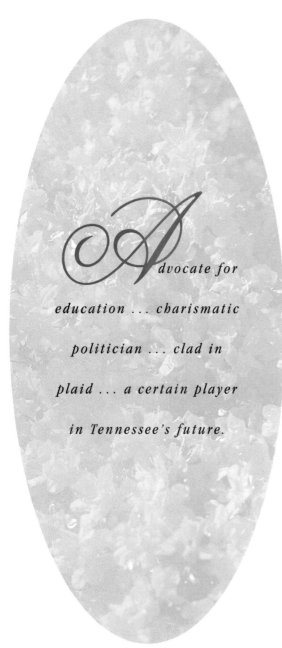

*A*dvocate for

education ... charismatic

politician ... clad in

plaid ... a certain player

in Tennessee's future.

Lamar and Honey Alexander

Fresh Tomatoes, Basil and Croutons with Thin Spaghetti

Honey Alexander discovered this recipe in a magazine a few years ago. She says, "It's quick and delicious and terrific at the cabin when the tomatoes are coming in and the basil is thriving! If there is any left over, it's great for lunch the next day."

¼	cup melted unsalted butter
4	large cloves of garlic, minced
4	cups cubed Italian or French bread
	Salt to taste
4	large tomatoes, coarsely chopped
1	clove of garlic, minced
½	jalapeño, minced (optional)
16	ounces thin spaghetti, cooked al dente
¼	cup olive oil
	Pepper to taste
2	cups chopped fresh basil

Preheat the oven to 400 degrees.

Combine the butter and 4 garlic cloves in a bowl. Add bread cubes, tossing to coat. Spread on a baking sheet.

Bake for 10 minutes or until golden brown. May season with salt.

Combine the tomatoes, 1 garlic clove and the jalapeño in a large bowl, tossing to mix.

Add the spaghetti and sprinkle with the olive oil. Toss to coat. Add salt, pepper, basil and half the croutons, tossing well.

Serve with the remaining croutons, fresh bread and a green salad.

yields four servings

Charismatic politician Lamar Alexander is famous for his 1978 walk across Tennessee in his bid for governor of the state, a position he held from 1979 to 1986. He then served as President of the University of Tennessee from 1988 to 1991, and as United States Secretary of Education under President George Bush. He is currently campaigning for Republican candidature as President of the United States and is Tennessee's choice for the future.

Stay-At-Home Tuesday Night Pasta

This is my original recipe.

5	cloves of garlic, finely chopped
2	medium Vidalia onions, chopped
2	tablespoons extra-virgin cold-pressed olive oil
5	green bell peppers, chopped
5	large tomatoes, chopped
1	bunch cilantro, chopped
	Salt and pepper to taste
1	(16-ounce) package spaghetti or other pasta
	Dried red chiles, chopped (optional)

Sauté the garlic and onions in the olive oil in a large skillet until lightly browned.

Add the green peppers, tomatoes, cilantro, salt and pepper.

Cook, covered, over medium heat until the green peppers are tender-crisp, stirring occasionally.

Cook the pasta using package directions; drain.

Toss the pasta with the vegetables in a large bowl. Top with the chiles if desired.

yields six servings

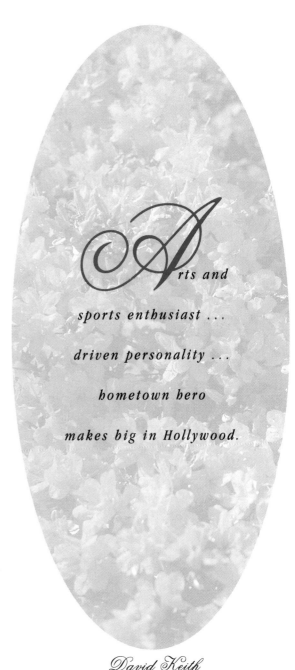

Arts and sports enthusiast ... driven personality ... hometown hero makes big in Hollywood.

Hometown hero David Keith was born and raised in Knoxville. A graduate of the University of Tennessee with a B.A. in speech and theater, he received an equity card from UT's Clarence Brown Company. Keith has starred in "The Great Santini," "An Officer and a Gentleman," and "Lords of Discipline," to name a few. In addition to his motion picture work, David has also performed on stage and has made his directoral debut. He maintains residences in Knoxville and Los Angeles and can often be seen on the sidelines of UT's football and basketball games.

David Keith

233

Napkins, Knives & Knoxville

Fried Green Tomatoes

Fried green tomatoes are a favorite in Dolly Parton's family. Here's her mama's recipe:

Slice green tomatoes and season with salt and pepper. Dip the slices into beaten egg mixture. Roll the slices in flour and fry in oil or bacon grease until browned.

Special thanks to Dolly's sister Willadeane for sharing this Parton family favorite.

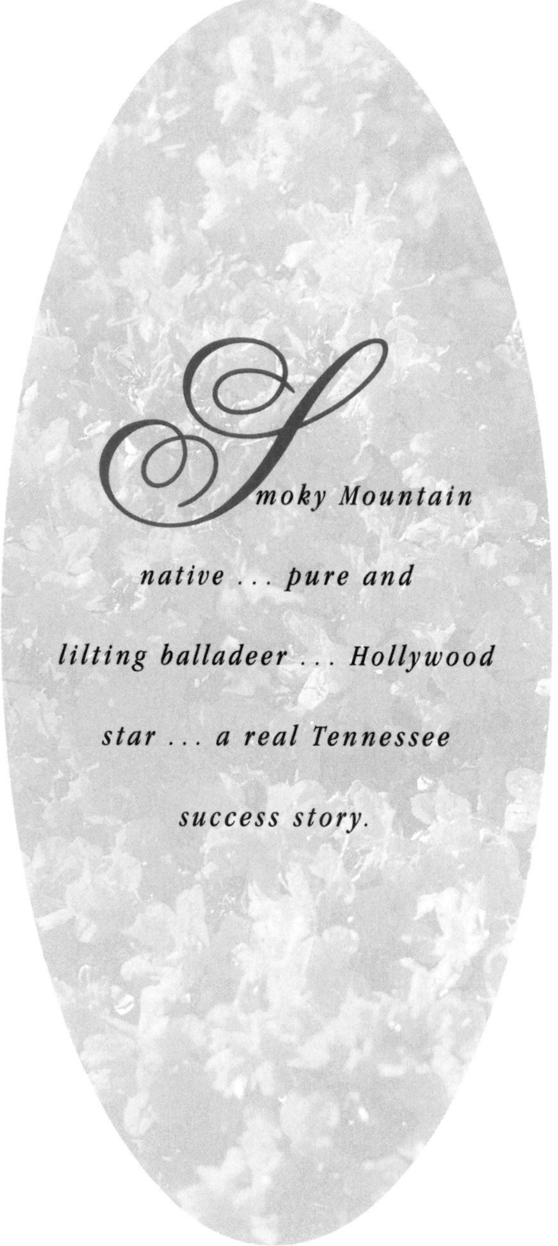

Dolly Parton grew up in rural Sevier County in the midst of the Smoky Mountain traditions that fill her songs. She left her home at age eighteen with her guitar, and went to Nashville. After receiving her first break with Porter Waggoner, Dolly rose to the top of the country and pop charts as singer and songwriter. Her movie credits include *The Best Little Whorehouse in Texas, Nine to Five,* and *Steel Magnolias.*

Smoky Mountain native ... pure and lilting balladeer ... Hollywood star ... a real Tennessee success story.

Dolly Parton

Our Friend's Chocolate-Mint Dessert

This is called "Our Friend's" because we stole the recipe from one of our friends, who undoubtedly stole it from another friend.

1	cup semisweet chocolate chips
1	cup miniature marshmallows
1	cup evaporated milk
½	cup butter or margarine
1	cup flour
¼	cup packed brown sugar
½	cup chopped pecans
½	gallon peppermint or mint-chocolate chip ice cream, softened

Combine the chocolate chips, marshmallows and evaporated milk in a medium saucepan.

Heat over low heat until the chocolate chips are melted, stirring frequently. Remove from the heat and let cool.

Cut the butter into the flour with a pastry blender in a large bowl until the mixture is crumbly. Stir in the brown sugar and pecans. Press the mixture onto a 10x14-inch baking sheet.

Bake at 400 degrees for 10 to 12 minutes or until lightly browned.

Crumble the baked mixture and press into a greased 8x8-inch baking pan, reserving 2 tablespoons for topping.

Spread half of the ice cream over the crumb crust. Top with half of the chocolate mixture. Spread with the remaining ice cream and chocolate mixture. Top with the reserved crumbs.

Freeze until firm.

yields twelve servings

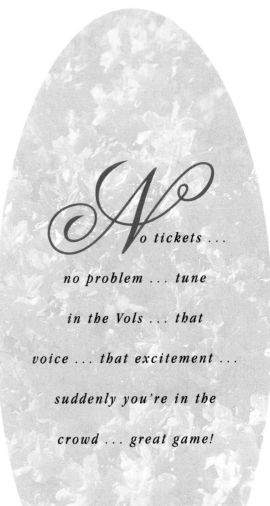

No tickets . . . no problem . . . tune in the Vols . . . that voice . . . that excitement . . . suddenly you're in the crowd . . . great game!

John Ward

John Ward is known as the "Voice of the Vols." He has been broadcasting Big Orange basketball for thirty years and Big Orange football for twenty-seven years. He has been honored as Sportscaster of the Year in Tennessee twenty-four times, and is a member of the Tennessee Sports Hall of Fame.

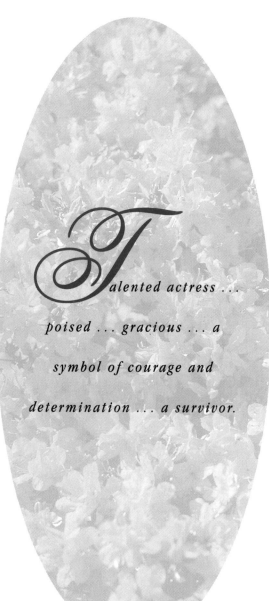

T alented actress ...

poised ... gracious ... a

symbol of courage and

determination ... a survivor.

Patricia Neal

Carrot Cake with Cream Cheese Icing

2	cups sugar
1	cup vegetable oil
4	eggs, beaten
2	cups flour
½	teaspoon salt
1	teaspoon baking powder
2	teaspoons baking soda
2	tablespoons cinnamon
¼	cup water
2	cups grated carrots
½	cup butter, softened
8	ounces cream cheese, softened
1	(l-pound) package confectioners' sugar
⅛	teaspoon salt
2	teaspoons vanilla extract
1	cup chopped pecans

Mix the sugar, oil and eggs in a large bowl, beating until smooth.

Mix the flour, salt, baking powder, baking soda and cinnamon together. Add to the egg mixture gradually, stirring well. Add the water and carrots. Pour the batter into a greased and floured bundt pan or a 9½x13-inch cake pan.

Bake at 325 degrees for 45 minutes. Remove to a wire rack to cool.

Cream the butter and cream cheese in a medium bowl until light and fluffy. Add confectioners' sugar, salt and vanilla, stirring well. Fold in pecans. Spread mixture over cooled cake.

yields ten servings

Patricia Neal, Oscar-winning actress, moved to Knoxville as a young girl and graduated from Knoxville High School. She was an apprentice at Barter Theater in 1942, and four years later she received a Tony Award for her role in "Another Part of the Forest." Patricia was at the peak of her acting career when she suffered a series of strokes in 1965 that left her partially paralyzed. Through years of rehabilitation she fought to regain her independence so she could resume her career. In 1977, the Fort Sanders Regional Medical Center dedicated the Patricia Neal Rehabilitation Center in her honor as a stroke survivor. Patricia has been committed to the development of the Center, which she affectionately calls her "House of Heroes." It stands as a symbol to her courage and determination.

Dirt Cake

This is not a recipe I came up with, but I enjoy making it and it looks just like a dirt-filled flower pot. For more fun, you may also add a few "gummy worms" to the top. If you use a clay flower pot, do not wash it, because the clay absorbs water, but do clean and bake it at 350 degrees for 20 minutes. It is best to use a plastic flower pot.

1	(20-ounce) package chocolate sandwich cookies
½	cup butter, softened
8	ounces cream cheese, softened
½	cup confectioners' sugar
2	(4-ounce) packages vanilla instant pudding mix
3½	cups milk
12	ounces whipped topping

∾ Process the cookies in a blender until finely crumbled or remove cream filling and finely crush with a rolling pin. Set aside.

∾ Cream the butter, cream cheese and confectioners' sugar in a medium bowl until light and fluffy.

∾ Beat the pudding mix and milk in a large bowl. Fold in the whipped topping. Add the cream cheese mixture, mixing thoroughly.

∾ Line a flower pot with aluminum foil. Alternate layers of cookie crumbs and pudding mixture until all ingredients are used, beginning and ending with cookie crumbs.

∾ Chill until serving time.

yields ten servings

Commanding presence ... winning spirit ... Olympic talent ... strike up the band ... another victory.

Pat Head Summitt

Pat Head Summitt has been the head coach of the University of Tennessee Lady Vols basketball team since 1973. She has led her teams to three national championships and reached the 500-win mark in 1994. Pat was co-captain of the 1976 Olympic silver medal basketball team and coached the 1984 Olympic team to a gold medal. She was named as Naismith College Coach of the Year in 1987, 1989, and 1994.

Mrs. Ruth's Famous Chocolate Pie

Mrs. Ruth Clayton, mother of Jim Clayton, has been preparing this Clayton family favorite dessert for 67 years. According to Kay Clayton, Jim's wife, this pie is famous in the Clayton clan, and Kay is lucky to enjoy a piece of this marvelous pie when other family members are around. Ruth always serves her special chocolate pie on holidays and when she knows her son Jim is joining her for dinner.

1¼   cups plus 2 tablespoons sugar
⅓   cup flour
1¼   tablespoons baking cocoa
1¼   cups milk
2   tablespoons margarine
1   teaspoon (plus) vanilla extract
2   egg yolks
1   baked (9-inch) pie shell
2   egg whites

Combine 1¼ cups of the sugar, flour and baking cocoa in a saucepan. Add the milk, stirring well. Cook over low heat until the sugar melts and the mixture thickens, stirring constantly. Stir in the margarine and 1 teaspoon vanilla. Beat the egg yolks in a small bowl. Add gradually to the cooked mixture, beating constantly. Pour the mixture into the prepared pie shell.

Bake at 350 degrees for 10 minutes.

Beat the egg whites with the remaining 2 tablespoons sugar and 2 or 3 drops of vanilla in a mixer bowl until stiff peaks form. Spread over the pie filling. Bake until brown.

Bake for 5 minutes longer, or until the meringue is lightly browned. Cool before serving.

yields six servings

Skilled

entrepreneur ... fulfiller

of dreams ... committed

to the arts ... and

the community ... a

true visionary.

Jim Clayton

Jim Clayton was born in Finger, Tennessee. He graduated from the University of Tennessee with a B.S. in electrical engineering and received his J.D. degree from UT as well. Early in his career, Jim was an engineer with WATE-TV. Several years later, he obtained a Volvo and other automobile franchises. From 1960 to 1976, Jim was the producer and host of the TV show Clayton's "Star Time." Jim is probably best known as the founder, CEO, and president of Clayton Homes, a Knoxville-based company which builds, retails, finances, and insures manufactured homes. Clayton Homes has received numerous honors from "Forbes" magazine, has been listed among the Business Week 1000 Corporate Elite since 1991, and is quoted on the New York Stock Exchange.

Pecan Pie

This is my favorite recipe because my mother used to make it for me when I was a little boy. Even the most fanatic Volunteer fans will take "time out" for this southern tradition.

1 ¾	cups sugar
¼	cup dark corn syrup
¼	cup butter or margarine
3	eggs
1	cup chopped pecans
¼	teaspoon salt
1	teaspoon vanilla extract
1	(unbaked) 9-inch pie shell

Combine the sugar, corn syrup and butter in a medium saucepan.

Cook over medium-high heat until the mixture begins to boil, stirring constantly. Remove from the heat.

Beat the eggs in a large bowl.

Add the hot syrup mixture 1 tablespoon at a time to the eggs, beating constantly.

Stir in the pecans, salt and vanilla.

Pour the mixture into the pie shell.

Bake at 375 degrees for 35 to 40 minutes or until a knife inserted near the center comes out clean.

yields six servings

A cold snap in the air . . .

95,000 fans . . . Offense . . .

Defense . . . a

Big Orange phenomenon!

Phil Fulmer served for thirteen years as an assistant coach of the University of Tennessee football team and was named head coach in 1992. He also played football for the Vols from 1968 to 1971.

Phil Fulmer

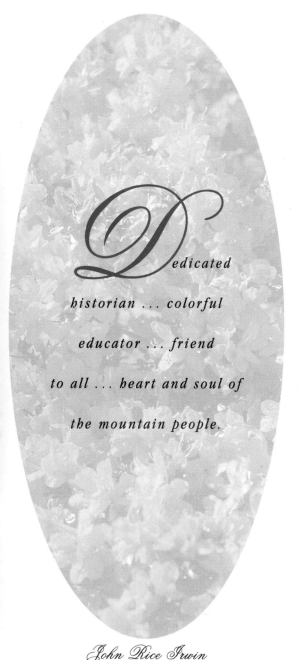

Baked Onions

When I have to prepare my own victuals, I grab whatever vegetables are available from the garden or pantry and put them to cooking. One day I happened to throw some onions in the oven to bake, to supplement boiled corn, fried okra, and corn bread. They turned out pretty good, and baked onions are now my claim to fame in the culinary world.

> Unpeeled mature onions
> Salt to taste
> Butter to taste

Bake the onions, skins and all, in a preheated 425-degree oven until totally mushy when stuck with a fork. An egg-sized onion will need to bake about 50 minutes; a baseball-sized onion takes from 60 to 75 minutes. Serve "as is." Each person should cut off the root end, then press gently with a knife or spoon while holding the onion in place with a fork until the onion pops out of the skin. Add salt and butter to the steaming onion.

Alex (Haley) always liked to illustrate to guests the proper method of removing the onion and I'm not sure which he enjoyed the most, extracting the onions, or eating them.

Mention regional historic preservation in East Tennessee and the work of John Rice Irwin instantly comes to mind. Over the years he has collected thousands of early-Tennessee artifacts and transformed them into a working museum, the Museum of Appalachia. Every year visitors from near and far gather at the Anderson County site for yearly celebrations, which feature artisans demonstrating discarded and near-forgotten skills and crafts. Amid the log cabins, one-room schoolhouse, and antique-exhibits building, special guests from every walk of life have participated in the experience of going back into Tennessee's cultural beginnings. ▶

Dedicated historian ... colorful educator ... friend to all ... heart and soul of the mountain people.

John Rice Irwin

Farm animals wander about portions of the tree-filled grounds, which are sectioned and fronted by weathered split rail fencing, and it was nearby that writer Alex Haley built his home. Not far down the highway, on the same deer trail that runs to the base of TVA's Norris Dam, is the old grist mill that John Rice's grandfather once operated and which today still occasionally is used to grind corn for meal. It's not surprising, then, that a recipe for corn bread is one of his contributions to the cookbook. A former educator in the public school system, an author, and a historian, John Rice and his wife Elizabeth have shared his corn bread and baked onions with celebrity guests such as Brooke Shields, Quincy Jones, Oprah Winfrey, Jane Fonda, and Lamar Alexander, and he has stories to tell about their preferences for these "lowly" dishes over more skillfully prepared ones.

Corn Bread

I mean no disrespect but I have never had what I thought was real corn bread served in a restaurant. Eggs, flour, sugar, etc., are for cakes, not corn bread, and maybe that's where restaurants go awry.

2	tablespoons corn oil
2	cups white corn meal mix
1¾	cups skim milk

Place corn oil in a 10-inch cast-iron skillet and heat in a preheated 450-degree oven for 5 minutes. Mix corn meal and milk in bowl, stirring thoroughly to ensure a good corn bread. Pour hot oil into batter and stir again. Pour batter into skillet. Bake for 30 minutes or until top is browned. Invert skillet to remove corn bread. Crumble leftovers in a glass of cold milk. Or slice cold bread and bake or fry in oil until crumb side is brown and crunchy.

While growing up in rural East Tennessee we had corn bread every day—except Sunday, when we served our company and our city relatives from Knoxville Merita light bread. The women in my family made great corn bread, but instead of measuring ingredients, they proceeded by grabs, pinches, and intuition.

The heavy iron skillet will drive the heat into the bread and result in a thick but crunchy crust. The bread pan should never be washed, only wiped clean of crumbs, and this will prevent the bread from sticking. It should always fall freely from the pan when the pan is turned upside down.

John Rice Irwin

Acknowledgements

Cookbook Taskforce 1994–1995

Debra Francisco Cuningham, *Chairman*

Paige von Hoffmann Anderson, *Text & Copywriting*

Karen Crawford Braden, *Recipe Testing Coordinator*

Emily Norman Cox, *Creative Coordinator*

Elizabeth Grayson Ellis, *Creative Coordinator*

Elizabeth Sharp Henderson, *Editorial Coordinator*

Susan Crowe Henry, *Recipe Development Coordinator*

Cindy Hopkins Milner, *Financial Coordinator*

Dee Bagwell Haslam, *1994–1995 President*

Cookbook Committee 1995–1996

Debra Francisco Cuningham, *Chairman*

Tonna Truesdell Heath, *Assistant Chairman*

Paige von Hoffmann Anderson, *Text & Copywriting*

Cindy Hopkins Milner, *Treasurer*

Laura Roberts Wright, *Assistant Treasurer*

Karen Crawford Braden, *Recipe Testing Coordinator*

Emily Norman Cox, *Creative Coordinator*

Elizabeth Grayson Ellis, *Creative Coordinator*

Elizabeth Sharp Henderson, *Editorial Coordinator*

Susan Crowe Henry, *Recipe Development Coordinator*

Susan Hopkins Long, *Marketing*

Jo Wilkerson Wetherall, *Assistant Marketing*

Michelle Brakebill, *Props Chairman*

Sue Patterson Dilworth, *Props Chairman*

Meg Cifers Manning, *Preview Party*

Beth Johnson Boatner, *Distribution*

Maggie Sheridan, *Distribution*

Kirsten Dahlberg Turner, *Distribution*

Kimberly Hull Reid, *Non-Credit*

Jacque Lintner McMurry, *Non-Credit*

Mari Firle Brooks, *1995–1996 President*

Contributors & Testers

The Junior League of Knoxville salutes its members who gave countless hours of recipe collection and testing in order to make this cookbook a reality.

Marie Fowler Alcorn
Melanie Horton Amburn
Paige von Hoffmann Anderson
Pam Arnett
Patti Wasmansdorff Arnold
Tere Gaut Atwater
Midge Orr Ayres
Ann Haslam Bailey
Penne Henley Baugh
Katie Bell
Merri Spaugh Biggs
Sandie Kohlhase Bishop
Beth Johnson Boatner
Ann McCabe Bodie
Sharon Bosse
Nancy Buchanan Bosson
Karen Crawford Braden
Jocelyn Rynes Brodd
Mari Firle Brooks
Cassandra Johnson Brownlow
Kathleen Brink Bullock
Marcy Wolpert Bunn
Pam Broughton Bustamante
Anne McCoin Callaway
Sara Nash Cantrell
Amy Stevenson Cathey
Ellyn Clapp Cauble
Sherry Flecken Chobanian
Donna McNab Cobble
Penny Pratt Cole
Conni Hanson Collins
Cindy Oakes Connor
Mindy Meredith Coulter
Emily Norman Cox
Debra Francisco Cuningham

Barbara Elder Davies
Joan Black Davis
Beverly Boge Dawson
Jan Black Deaderick
Molly Gunn Deuschle
Noel McCluskey Dill
Eleanor Roehl Dorrycott
Jeannie Hale Dulaney
Sheridan Anglea Dulaney
Jet Powell Dunlap
Elizabeth Grayson Ellis
Maribeth Ergen
Jody Connor Fair
Susan Additon Farris
Jane Rogers Feaster
Laura Leigh Finley
Betsy Guinn Foster
Leslie Grossman Frederick
Peggy McCready Fulton
Cheryl Tucker Gentry
Amy Kay Gibson
Melissa Cooley Gill
Bettye Gay Gilreath
Cammy Dean Glover
Susan Commons Goble
Ginger Gentry Gross
Carol Cline Gross
Gail Donohue Grossman
Penn Ervin Grove
Jane Smethells Gulley
Terri Phillipy Hale
Margo Stowers Hall
Jane Johnston Harb
Kelly Wilford Harb
Holly Harris
Crissy Garrett Haslam
Dee Bagwell Haslam
Sally Smith Hayes
Lane Schreeder Hays
Tonna Truesdell Heath
Elizabeth Sharp Henderson

Ruth Ann Sharp Henry
Susan Crowe Henry
Sally Leach Hester
Beverly Binkley Hogin
Jennifer Holder
Jill Chianese Hoover
Frances Curtis Howe
Jane Barefoot Hunter
Connie Henderson Hutchins
Ann Stubblefield Ince
Vickers Demetrio Johnson
Cynthia Attaway Jones
Margy Cooley Jones
Chris Brown Kahn
Kelley Canada Karnes
Lynn Schwarzenberg Keen
Harriet Jones Keener
Brenda Boaz Kelly
Lynda Herndon Kennedy
Donna Dahlen Kerr
Helen Weaver Kirk
Fannie Kleitches Kotsianas
Sarah Hardrath Kramer
Vandy Cifers Leake
Chris Lee
Kim Lindsay
Abigail Lawrence Lipsey
Malinda Carlen Little
Sandy Metrione Love
Randy Canada MacDonald
Catherine Ashe Maloy
Meg Cifers Manning
Glo Nelson Marquis
Deborah Massengale
Katherine Rodgers Mayfield
Melissa Gallivan McAdams
Kiki Link McCammon
Dale Reid McCarley
Carol Brumley McGlothlin
Mary Frances Hannan Merwin
Judy Warwick Miller

Nancy Rice Miller
Cindy Hopkins Milner
Mary Beth Cranwell Montgomery
Beverly Burdick Morton
Lauralie MacRae Morton
Suzanne Smith Moyer
Geri Carmichael Muse
Cornelia Shirley Norman
Sande Holland Novick
Teedee Garland Nystrom
Anne Walters Pittenger
Nancy Orr Preston
Nancy Newberry Prosser
Denise Moore Purnell
Virginia Pert Rainwater
Kimberly Hull Reid
Barbara Rentenbach
Sallee Hendrickson Reynolds
Carol Richards
Pamela Young Richardson
Hanley Testerman Roach
Beverly Broadwater Roberts
Gloria Tolmie Robertson
Marilyn Long Roddy
Marilyn Seay Roehl
Becky Wiltcher Rohde
Lois Haws Ross
Sheryl Mitchell Sampson
Rusha Kinard Sams
Cherly Lima Sanders
Malissa Reagan Scruggs
Georgia Walker Seagren
Maggie Sheridan
Mary Jo Richards Shires
Kelle Reneau Shultz
Nancy Julian Siler
Susan Reeder Siler
Debra Simerly
Ethel Baumann Skaggs
DeAnna Bowlin Slagle
Caroline Manchton Smith

Ellen Clarke Spitzer
Grayce Fox Stair
Mary Harris Straight
Leslie Coffin Swift
Jeanne May Tapp
Sabra Claiborne Tatum
Sheryl Dawson Taylor
Janice Guion Threlkeld
Rosemary Morris Trimble
Danni Bowers Varlan
Kendra S. Walker
Sue Gray Walker
Kim Stewart Walling
Leslie Hull Welsch
Jo Wilkerson Wetherall
Shelley Sandlin White
Karen Harr White
Diane Wright Wilkes
Susan Weyrauch Williams
Frankie Mayo Williams
Carolyn Harang Winder
Jeanne Atkins Wolfe
Carmita Haller Wright
Cathy Hill Youmans
Jo Murphy Zarger

Bibliography

Thank You

The Junior League of Knoxville wishes to express a very special thank you to the following friends and businesses who donated their time, their homes, and their expertise to the production of this cookbook.

Andrew Morton Gifts

Ashe's Wines & Spirits

Braden's Wholesale Furniture

The Flower Market

The Inn at Blackberry Farm

Sassafras Polo Club

The White Lily Foods Company

Mr. and Mrs. Charles Anderson

Molly Bland

Cassandra Johnson Brownlow

Mr. and Mrs. John Turner Dawson, Jr.

Missy Shofner Flaherty

Susan Commons Goble

Dr. and Mrs. Paul Googe

Mr. and Mrs. Art Grayson

Dr. and Mrs. Allan Grossman

Mr. and Mrs. James A. Haslam, III

Mr. Campbell Howard

Vickers Demetrio Johnson

Randy Canada MacDonald

Jack Neely

Mr. and Mrs. Ralph V. Norman, Jr.

Mr. and Mrs. William N. Parsons

Debra Swanson

Judy Toline

Cathy Hill Youmans

Bibliography

"A diva comes home." Barbara Aston-Wash. *Knoxville News Sentinel*, October, 1994.

Alexander, Lamar. *Six Months Off: An American Family's Australian Adventure.* New York, NY: William Morrow and Co., Inc., 1988.

Chalmers, Irena. *The Great Food Almanac: A Feast of Facts from A to Z.* San Francisco, CA: Collins Publishers, ©1994.

Duncan, David. *Cooking with David Duncan.* Knoxville, TN: The Pullman Press, 1990.

Dykeman, Wilma. * *Explorations.* Nashville, TN: American Association for State and Local History, 1984.

Dykeman, Wilma. * *Tennessee, A History*: New York, NY: W.W. Norton & Company, Inc., 1975.

Hughs, Ina. *A Prayer for Children.* New York, NY: William Morrow and Co., Inc., 1995.

Martin, Laura C. *Folklore of Trees and Shrubs.* Chester, CT: Globe Pequot Press, ©1992

Martin, Laura C. *Folklore of Wildflowers.* Chester, CT: Globe Pequot Press, © 1994

Neal, Patricia with Richard DeNeut. *As I Am: An Autobiography.* New York, NY: Simon and Schuster, 1988, 85-86.

Parton, Dolly. *Dolly: My Life and Other Unfinished Business.* New York, NY: Harper Collins Publishing, Inc., 1994.

* Page references for quotations from Wilma Dykeman are as follows in order of appearance: *Explorations* pages 4-5, 229, 235, 234, 5, 238, 142, 59, 229, 5, 126 and 75-76. *Tennessee, A History* pages 4, 8, 8, 8 and 11.

Nutritional Profile Guidelines

The editors have attempted to present these family recipes in a form that allows approximate nutritional values to be computed. Persons with dietary or health problems or whose diets require close monitoring should not rely solely on the nutritional information provided. They should consult their physicians or a registered dietitian for specific information.

Abbreviations for Nutritional Profile

Cal—Calories	Fiber—Dietary Fiber	Sod—Sodium
Prot—Protein	T Fat—Total Fat	g—grams
Carbo—Carbohydrates	Chol—Cholesterol	mg—milligrams

Nutritional information for these recipes is computed from information derived from many sources, including materials supplied by the United States Department of Agriculture, computer databanks, and journals in which the information is assumed to be in the public domain. However, many specialty items, new products, and processed foods may not be available from these sources or may vary from the average values used in these profiles. More information on new and/or specific products may be obtained by reading the nutrient labels. Unless otherwise specified, the nutritional profile of these recipes is based on all measurements being level.

Artificial sweeteners vary in use and strength so should be used "to taste," using the recipe ingredients as a guideline. Sweeteners using aspartame (NutraSweet and Equal) should not be used as a sweetener in recipes involving prolonged heating, which reduces the sweet taste. For further information on the use of these sweeteners, refer to package.

Alcoholic ingredients have been analyzed for the basic ingredients, although cooking causes the evaporation of alcohol, thus decreasing caloric content.

• Buttermilk, sour cream, and yogurt are the types available commercially.

• Cake mixes which are prepared using package directions include 3 eggs and ½ cup oil.

• Chicken, cooked for boning and chopping, has been roasted; this method yields the lowest caloric values.

• Cottage cheese is cream-style with 4.2% creaming mixture. Dry curd cottage cheese has no creaming mixture.

• Eggs are all large. To avoid raw eggs that may carry salmonella, as in eggnog or 6-week muffin batter, use an equivalent amount of commercial egg substitute.

• Flour is unsifted all-purpose flour.

• Garnishes, serving suggestions, and other optional additions and variations are not included in the profile.

• Margarine and butter are regular, not whipped or presoftened.

• Milk is whole milk, 3.5% butterfat. Lowfat milk is 1% butterfat. Evaporated milk is whole milk with 60% of the water removed.

• Oil is any type of vegetable cooking oil. Shortening is hydrogenated vegetable shortening.

• Salt and other ingredients to taste as noted in the ingredients have not been included in the nutritional profile.

• If a choice of ingredients has been given, the nutritional profile reflects the first option. If a choice of amounts has been given, the nutritional profile reflects the greater amount.

Nutritional Information

Page No.	Recipe Title	No. Servings	Cal	Prot (g)	Carbo (g)	T Fat (g)	% Cal From Fat	Chol (mg)	Fiber (g)	Sod (mg)
					Approximate Per Serving					
16	Bruschetta Romano (per appetizer)	48	114	2	12	7	52	1	1	305
17	Cheese Straws (per appetizer)	48	99	3	6	7	64	10	<1	155
17	Crab-Stuffed Mushrooms (per appetizer)	12	33	4	2	1	26	14	<1	131
18	Egg Rolls	24	425	25	29	23	49	98	1	471
19	Focaccia Tomato Pie	16	Nutritional information for this recipe is not available.							
19	Goat Cheese with Olives and Sun-Dried Tomatoes	24	101	4	8	6	53	11	1	171
20	Spinach Pastry Roll-Ups	24	159	5	11	11	61	27	1	207
21	Artichoke Dip (per ounce)	40	45	2	1	4	75	7	<1	135
21	Sugar-and-Spice Pecans (per ounce)	40	111	1	8	9	70	0	1	30
22	Black Bean Dip (per ounce)	56	28	1	3	1	43	0	1	55
22	Baked Crab Dip (per ounce)	12	83	4	1	7	77	32	<1	104
23	Cheddar Cheese Ring (per ounce)	72	148	4	4	14	81	19	<1	132
23	Herb Cheese Spread	12	227	9	10	17	67	45	<1	226
24	Italian Torta	48	154	3	1	16	90	37	<1	136
25	Mushroom Pâté	12	75	1	2	7	85	21	<1	90
26	Salmon Pâté	16	90	4	1	7	70	26	<1	346
27	Shepherd Loaf	16	201	9	17	11	50	42	1	281
30	Famous White Lily Biscuits	12	121	3	16	5	37	2	1	272
31	Aloha Bread	24	306	3	35	18	51	27	1	132
32	Banana Date Bread	12	474	5	48	31	57	98	3	458
33	Oatmeal-Applesauce Bread	12	101	3	19	1	12	3	1	190
34	Orange-Glazed Cranberry-Pumpkin Bread	24	328	4	50	14	36	35	2	228
35	Pepperoni Bread	12	135	4	19	5	32	9	1	358
35	Melt-Away Yeast Rolls	24	137	3	18	6	40	9	1	334
36	Sour Cream Rolls	48	103	2	10	6	53	24	<1	77
37	Best Bread in the World	24	138	4	28	2	11	11	2	278
38	Poppy Seed Bread	24	281	3	41	12	38	29	1	170
39	Swedish Vittebröd	24	96	2	16	3	26	14	3	155
40	Oatmeal Muffins	12	173	3	21	9	45	18	1	386
40	Sweet Potato Muffins	36	60	1	10	2	32	10	<1	70
41	Corn Bread Muffins	18	93	3	13	3	32	<1	1	161
41	Texas Corn Bread	9	167	4	22	7	36	40	1	487
44	Chiles Rellenos	8	190	14	8	11	54	135	1	698
45	Crab and Egg Supreme	12	441	16	8	38	78	279	<1	770
46	Sausage Mushroom Breakfast Casserole	12	283	15	9	21	66	119	1	823
47	Zucchini and Sausage Quiche	8	393	15	16	31	70	156	1	592
48	Breakfast Pizza	8	349	17	21	22	57	156	<1	1015
49	Grits Soufflé	12	392	18	22	26	59	273	3	552
49	Tomato Pie	6	319	6	20	25	68	21	2	320

Page No.	Recipe Title	No. Servings	Cal	Prot (g)	Carbo (g)	T Fat (g)	% Cal From Fat	Chol (mg)	Fiber (g)	Sod (mg)
					Approximate Per Serving					
50	Banana Brunch Bread	12	385	5	47	21	48	81	1	302
51	Rise-and-Shine Coffee Cakes	12	306	4	31	19	55	79	1	203
52	Raspberry Cream Cheese Danish	8	289	4	38	14	44	29	1	466
53	Fruit Pizza	8	318	5	44	11	30	16	1	220
54	Apple Bake	8	355	2	60	14	34	34	4	42
55	Apple Butter (per ¼ cup)	24	70	<1	19	<1	1	0	2	20
55	Hot Fruit Compote	12	218	3	50	3	10	0	5	24
60	Orange Sherbet Salad	12	206	2	34	8	32	28	<1	62
61	Fruit Salad	8	295	3	45	24	73	160	2	21
62	Molded Gazpacho	8	140	5	12	10	57	0	3	1045
63	Cold Salmon Mousse with Cucumber Sauce	8	239	13	3	20	75	70	<1	277
64	Celebration Pasta Salad	4	873	28	91	44	46	25	4	887
65	Greek Orzo Salad	4	385	31	21	20	46	243	2	891
66	Barley Salad	12	173	3	21	10	48	0	3	346
67	Wild Rice Salad	12	204	4	25	10	44	0	1	276
68	German Potato Salad	8	294	10	45	9	27	16	3	312
68	Red Potato Salad	8	287	6	22	20	61	17	2	447
69	Mixed Greens with Bleu Cheese and Raspberry Vinaigrette	10	246	5	11	22	75	8	4	169
70	Mixed Greens with Warm Roquefort Dressing	12	201	7	6	18	76	31	2	408
71	Best-Ever Green Salad	6	598	11	28	51	75	25	2	409
72	Brutus Salad	6	380	10	11	34	78	17	1	597
72	Caesar Croutons	3	334	6	16	28	74	37	1	385
73	Roasted Garlic Caesar Salad	8	305	11	12	24	68	18	2	438
74	Spinach and Apple Salad	8	143	4	6	12	74	5	2	122
75	Strawberry-Spinach Salad	6	419	7	28	34	68	10	6	103
76	Poppy Seed Salad Dressing (per ounce)	16	163	<1	10	14	76	0	<1	134
76	Honey Dijon Salad Dressing (per ounce)	14	173	<1	6	17	86	9	0	204
77	Southern Cole Slaw Dressing (per ounce)	48	69	<1	4	6	79	2	<1	79
77	Tarragon Vinaigrette (per ounce)	8	146	<1	7	14	82	0	0	134
80	Asparagus and Artichokes	14	173	3	7	16	78	0	1	522
81	Carrots with Shiitake Mushrooms and Rosemary-Madeira Sauce	4	283	3	31	7	22	0	6	147
82	Kahlúa Glazed Carrots	6	94	1	16	2	19	5	3	48
83	Eggplant with Basil	6	239	12	10	17	63	45	4	217
84	Mushrooms au Gratin	8	179	7	8	14	67	36	2	244
85	Parmesan Potatoes	4	568	26	28	40	63	105	2	1169
86	Potato Gratiné	8	453	7	45	28	55	101	4	89
87	Spinach and Artichoke Casserole	12	191	12	21	9	40	11	5	447
88	Sweet Potato Casserole	8	427	4	55	23	47	36	3	217
89	Summer Vegetable Medley	6	169	7	14	10	48	12	3	359
90	Vegetable Mornay	8	267	5	12	23	74	25	1	690
91	Garden Medley	10	87	4	7	5	53	9	2	48
91	Neapolitan Tomato Sauce for Pasta	4	443	12	72	12	24	0	4	22
92	Rice with Pine Nuts	4	295	7	39	12	37	19	1	368
93	Marinated Tomatoes	8	103	1	5	9	78	0	1	276

Page No.	Recipe Title	No. Servings	Cal	Prot (g)	Carbo (g)	T Fat (g)	% Cal From Fat	Chol (mg)	Fiber (g)	Sod (mg)
94	Sauce and Topping for Green Vegetables (per ¼ cup)	8	118	3	3	11	80	18	<1	112
95	Pesto	6	314	9	30	18	51	4	2	195
100	Beef in Burgundy	8	744	38	44	37	45	132	2	539
101	Three-Day Brisket	24	222	25	6	10	43	83	<1	425
102	Bourbon Filets	4	696	47	5	47	60	236	1	407
103	Veal Scaloppine	2	965	55	42	53	50	220	2	821
104	Grilled Butterflied Leg of Lamb with Herbs	8	629	78	3	32	47	250	1	216
105	Marinated London Broil	6	309	37	6	14	41	90	1	1167
106	Madeira Sauce (per ounce)	10	33	1	2	2	53	5	<1	200
106	Barbecue Sauce (per ¼ cup)	24	62	<1	14	<1	3	0	<1	399
107	Grilled Pork Tenderloin	6	337	28	4	23	62	74	<1	1021
108	Chinese Pork Tenderloin	8	128	20	3	3	25	56	0	564
109	Baked Stuffed Pork Tenderloin	6	254	23	15	11	39	72	1	528
110	Stuffed Pizza	8	498	21	54	23	40	48	5	833
111	Boursin-Stuffed Chicken Breasts	8	344	30	9	20	53	120	<1	556
112	Peppered Chicken Breasts with Rosemary and Garlic	4	207	27	2	10	44	73	<1	64
113	Sherried Chicken Breasts	6	330	34	2	19	53	91	<1	659
114	Vermouth-Poached Chicken with Rice	6	415	41	34	9	20	106	2	1096
115	Chicken Marsala	4	271	32	21	4	13	73	<1	592
116	Chicken Pot Pie	4	655	35	46	36	50	120	7	592
117	Chicken Enchiladas	4	720	43	46	42	51	139	8	2993
118	Texas-Style Cornish Game Hens	6	537	52	23	26	44	166	1	1019
119	Elegant Orange Roughy	4	310	47	2	12	35	226	1	547
120	Marinated Grilled Tuna	8	247	28	2	13	46	45	<1	1074
121	Maryland Crab Cakes with Herb Mayonnaise	6	484	20	13	39	73	187	<1	1062
122	Lobster Linguini in Tomato Cream Sauce	4	885	44	102	34	35	192	7	1487
123	Cajun Seafood Carbonara	10	1099	51	78	64	52	301	3	2211
124	Sea Scallops Florentine	6	230	22	7	13	50	36	3	575
125	Shrimp Thermidor	4	760	30	17	62	73	429	1	1001
126	Ocean Spring Shrimp	4	489	30	7	38	70	314	1	723
127	Mustard Mint Sauce	8	185	<1	1	21	98	0	<1	75
127	Lemon-Chive Topping	1	76	<1	<1	8	98	5	0	63
130	Chilled Zucchini Soup	6	191	9	10	14	63	26	2	1188
131	Lentil Soup	20	162	10	25	3	17	8	4	438
132	Potato Soup	8	179	5	21	9	43	14	1	936
133	Jack-O'-Lantern Soup	9	252	7	26	13	44	14	4	391
134	Vegetable Soup	12	92	9	9	3	26	23	2	401
135	Chili	10	332	33	20	13	36	88	4	545
136	White Chicken Chili	6	437	39	52	9	18	58	15	977
137	Pink Chili	6	436	46	53	5	10	80	16	2038
138	Corn Chowder	10	313	6	29	20	57	58	3	681
139	Salmon Chowder	6	294	16	27	14	42	59	2	1148
140	Sherried Crab Bisque	6	247	20	8	15	55	116	1	508
141	Shrimp Bisque	4	410	19	14	31	66	207	1	916

Page No.	Recipe Title	No. Servings	Cal	Prot (g)	Carbo (g)	T Fat (g)	% Cal From Fat	Chol (mg)	Fiber (g)	Sod (mg)
							Approximate Per Serving			
142	Chicken Noodle Soup Mix	8	11	1	4	<1	15	7	<1	1081
143	Brunswick Stew	8	426	36	55	9	18	77	12	1697
144	Lamb Stew	6	368	43	17	14	34	129	5	292
145	Veal Stew Provençale	6	433	35	33	14	29	115	7	908
148	Baked Brie with Elephant Garlic	10	149	5	18	7	39	11	2	210
149	Sausage Cheese Puffs	48	79	3	5	5	62	8	<1	157
150	Tennessee Caviar	56	14	1	3	<1	9	<1	1	64
150	Big "O" Pretzels	6	163	5	34	<1	3	0	2	55
151	Black-Eyed Bean Salad	10	195	9	32	4	17	0	10	431
152	Chicken Salad Galore	20	410	15	25	29	62	49	2	208
153	Corn Bread Salad	12	486	15	42	31	55	46	4	1311
154	Marinated Green Beans	6	270	7	25	17	54	14	5	182
155	Grilled Marinated Flank Steak	6	312	22	7	20	58	52	1	939
156	Fried Chicken	4	688	62	67	18	24	167	3	6602
156	Ham Sandwiches	8	442	27	25	26	53	88	1	1195
157	Reuben Loaf	6	438	23	62	10	22	30	3	1938
158	Chocolate Truffles	60	113	1	14	6	49	8	<1	61
158	Touchdown Brownies	16	260	3	31	15	50	42	2	68
159	Cracker Candy	24	191	2	19	13	58	24	1	158
159	Orange Wassail	17	112	1	27	<1	3	0	1	3
164	Fruit Tea	16	85	<1	22	<1	<1	0	<1	3
164	Ginger Tea	16	135	<1	35	<1	1	0	<1	5
165	Plantation Almond Tea	4½	91	<1	24	<1	<1	0	<1	4
165	Holiday Wassail	16	188	1	47	<1	1	0	1	7
166	Hot Swedish Vinglögg	6	246	1	21	2	8	0	1	15
166	Cappuccino Mix	85	36	1	8	<1	2	1	<1	16
167	Spice Mix for Mulled Beverage	4	43	1	11	1	22	0	4	16
168	Crimson Punch	30	77	<1	11	<1	1	0	<1	4
168	Slush Punch	64	133	<1	34	<1	1	0	<1	13
169	Sparkling Champagne Punch	9	189	1	27	<1	1	0	<1	8
169	White Christmas Punch	56	233	2	43	7	25	27	<1	74
170	Minted Hot Cocoa	3	458	3	91	12	22	0	2	73
170	Irish Cream Liqueur	5	765	8	51	42	49	157	<1	145
171	The Perfect Oyster Shooter	12	196	5	6	1	5	25	0	166
171	The Quintessential Bloody Mary	1	185	2	14	<1	1	0	2	2842
174	Cream Puffs	12	421	8	44	25	53	150	1	327
175	Lemon Cream Freeze	8	429	2	47	28	56	102	<1	95
176	Chocolate Amaretto Cheesecake	8	822	13	54	60	65	255	1	596
177	Luscious Cheesecake	12	552	9	48	37	59	166	<1	358
178	Black Forest Cake	12	821	7	65	61	66	171	2	308
179	Blackstone Chocolate Satin Cake	16	563	5	60	36	54	133	4	190
180	Carrot Cake	12	827	8	112	40	43	20	1	590
181	Fresh Apple Cake	16	643	5	64	43	58	66	3	263
182	Caramel Applesauce Cake	12	720	7	100	35	43	132	3	457

Page No.	Recipe Title	Approximate Per Serving								
		No. Servings	Cal	Prot (g)	Carbo (g)	T Fat (g)	% Cal From Fat	Chol (mg)	Fiber (g)	Sod (mg)
184	Coca-Cola Cake	12	686	5	101	31	40	98	2	332
185	Holiday Cake	12	870	7	86	57	58	90	2	605
186	Hummingbird Cake	12	862	8	113	44	45	95	3	398
187	Chocolate Sour Cream Pound Cake	16	528	6	72	25	42	73	2	350
188	Cream Cheese Pound Cake	12	614	8	75	32	47	127	1	356
189	Lavender Pound Cake	16	314	5	44	14	38	98	1	179
190	Apple Sheet Pie	50	222	2	25	13	53	7	2	55
191	Buttermilk Pie	8	482	5	66	23	42	112	1	340
191	Peaches-and-Cream Pie	8	341	3	41	19	49	41	1	134
192	Strawberry Chiffon Pie	8	308	5	41	15	41	113	1	288
193	Coconut Caramel Pies	16	488	7	48	31	56	44	3	381
194	Fresh Fruit Tart	8	404	5	36	28	61	63	2	230
195	Pear Almond Tart	8	486	7	70	22	38	58	6	13
196	Tennessee Pecan Pie	8	586	6	57	40	59	111	2	312
197	Blackberry Cobbler	8	598	6	78	30	45	0	7	312
198	"Out of-This-League" Brownies	15	355	6	36	23	55	47	3	180
199	Date-Nut Bars	15	152	1	21	8	44	31	1	114
200	Ginger Cookies	40	90	1	14	4	36	5	<1	71
201	Lemon Sugar Cookies	48	157	2	21	8	43	18	<1	36
202	Holiday Shortbread	15	285	3	35	15	47	47	1	130
203	Chocolate Almond Biscotti	28	175	3	23	9	44	24	1	72

Index

Order Form

Name: _____ Address: _____

City: _____ State: _____ Zip: _____

Telephone: (_____) _____

COOKBOOK	PRICE	QUANTITY		TOTAL PRICE
Dining in the Smoky Mountain Mist	$21.95	x _____	=	_____
The Pear Tree (Holiday Recipes)	$4.95	x _____	=	_____
		Subtotal	=	_____
Dining in the Smoky Mountain Mist		Shipping & Handling $3.50 (per book)	+	_____
The Pear Tree		Shipping & Handling $1.75 (per book)	+	_____
		Subtotal	=	_____
		TN Residents add 8.25% Sales Tax	=	_____
		Total Enclosed	=	_____

Method of Payment ❏ Check ❏ Money Order ❏ VISA ❏ MasterCard

Account Number: _____ Expiration Date: _____

Signature: _____

Profits from the sale of these cookbooks are returned to the community through the Junior League of Knoxville projects.

Send check or money order to:

JUNIOR LEAGUE OF KNOXVILLE
P.O. Box 11632
Knoxville, Tennessee 37939
(423) 523-0350
FAX: (423) 522-4852